Sue Kreitzman's
Low-Fat
Vegetarian
Cookbook

Also by Sue Kreitzman
and published by Piatkus

The Complete Low-Fat Cookbook

The Quick After-Work Low-Fat Cookbook

Sue Kreitzman's
Low-Fat
Vegetarian
Cookbook

PIATKUS

For Natty Bumpo
and
Vicki Kimm

First published in 1994 by
Judy Piatkus (Publishers) Ltd
5 Windmill Street, London W1P 1HF

First paperback edition 1996, reissued 1998

*A catalogue record for this book is available
from the British Library*

ISBN 0-7499-1415-7 (Hbk)
0-7499-1910-8 (Pbk)

Photographs by James Murphy
Food prepared by Janet Smith
Styling by Jane McLeish
Text designed by Bridgewater Books

Typeset by Computerset, Harmondsworth
Printed and bound by Bookcraft (Bath) Ltd

Cover photograph shows Acorn Squash stuffed with Mushroom Ragout (page 167)
and Butternut Squash stuffed with Sweet Rice Pulau (page 60)

Contents

· · · · · · · · · ● · · · · · · · ·

Acknowledgements

Thank you so much to Sandie Mitchel-King who tackled the manuscript on short notice, enabled me to meet a demanding deadline (you want it *when*?!) and sailed through the whole thing with her usual competence and aplomb.

Thanks too, to my son Shawm who showed up unexpectedly at my front door just when I needed him the most, and to my husband Steve who keeps me nutritionally correct.

I am grateful to Snakehall Farm (The Prospect Trust) for supplying incomparable vegetables in season and to their garden team for keeping my garden bristling with herbs.

And finally, thank you to David Grossman who managed to pull me out of the doldrums, Vicki Kimm who cares deeply about vegetarianism, and is always happy to talk about (vegan) food, and to Brenda Huebler who – as always – helps in many ways.

Introduction

The joy of vegetarian eating is in its dazzling variety. The beans, the grains, the vegetables, the herbs; if you find culinary possibility exciting, then each time you plan a meal, the excess of it all can drive you into a frenzy. For meat-eaters, it is all too easy to fall into a well-worn rut of fish and chips, sausages and mash, or meat and two veg (one of them invariably potato). Vegetarians, on the other hand, seem willing to explore the whole world of cuisine.

A vegetarian lifestyle is easier now than it has ever been. Luxurious choice is available in all aspects of the vegetarian diet. Beans, for instance, range from the humble red kidney through to the black-eyed, the borlotti, the pinto, the cannellini and several varieties of lentils and split peas, all the way up to the noble turtle (or black) bean. And grains? The choice begins with plain rice, and continues through couscous, bulghur, barley, millet, polenta, right up to wild rice. If the supermarket hasn't got what you want (although it often has) the wholefood shop will. And that's not all: let's not forget the vegetables themselves. These days, greengrocery departments are botanical bazaars of delight. Comforting roots and potatoes; fascinating fennel and kohlrabi; elegant asparagus and aubergine; succulent sugar snap peas; crisphead, radicchio, rocket; multi-varieties of mushrooms; green, yellow, red and orange peppers – browsing along the shelves is pure delight.

The aim of this book is to help you harness all this glory into a low-fat way of life. Curtailing your dietary fat levels does not mean that you have to curtail your gastronomic pleasure as well. Nor will you need to exist on tiny portions; one of the advantages of a very low-fat lifestyle is that you will be able to eat large amounts, in fact you *should* do so, for the sake of adequate nutrition. You will be able to take advantage of our modern-day food supply, and eat a wide and interesting variety of foods.

A Low–Fat Lifestyle

There are many reasons for switching to a low-fat diet: to lose some excess weight, to get off the dieting 'yo-yo', to reduce cholesterol levels, to alleviate other medical problems that specifically require minimal dietary fat levels, or just to enjoy the benefits of a healthier way of eating.

If, as many people do these days, you replace highly saturated fats, such as butter, with highly monounsaturated or polyunsaturated fats, such as olive or sunflower oil, or the artificially resaturated fats in margarines (unsaturated fats are liquid at room temperature and have to be 'resaturated' to make a spreadable margarine), then you have not adopted a low-fat lifestyle, you have simply switched from one kind of fat to another. If you need to lose weight or maintain weight loss; if, for medical reasons, you must keep your fat intake to an absolute minimum; if you just want to improve the quality of your diet and enable yourself to eat large portions without ballooning into obesity, then you must cut right down on *all* fats.

There are three components of food that provide calories: protein, carbohydrate and fat (including *oils*, which are simply fat in liquid form). Fat provides more than twice the calories of protein and carbohydrate. The latter two provide 4 Calories per gram each, while fat provides 9 Calories per gram. In practical terms, this works out at about 120 Calories per tablespoon of fat. And not only is fat much higher in calories, it is also metabolised differently: dietary fat goes to body fat stores in an extremely quick and easy fashion. Moreover, diets high in fats and oils (highly saturated *and* highly unsaturated), have been implicated in various diseases (heart and artery disease, gall bladder problems, several kinds of cancer, to name but a few). It makes a lot of sense, therefore, both to help control weight and improve health, to cut right down on fat, but how exactly does one begin?

Making Changes

Skimmed Milk Products

Switch from whole milk dairy products to those made from skimmed milk. You will be surprised how quickly your palate accustoms itself to the change; in fact, after a while, whole milk products will seem unpleasantly fatty and cloying. There is a soul-satisfying profusion of useful skimmed-milk dairy products available in the supermarkets these days. Have you tried no-fat fromage frais? It's thick, creamy and luscious, and is great mixed with chopped fresh herbs, or – for a sweet treat – with a little honey or marmalade and the scrapings from a vanilla pod. Quark (it sounds like the cry of a drunken duck, but is actually a beautifully smooth, no-fat curd cheese) is outstandingly useful as well, as is no-fat yoghurt, especially if you drain it to make a compelling 'cream' cheese (see page 45). Buttermilk, thick as pouring cream, is cultured from skimmed milk, and has a myriad of uses. And skimmed milk itself, of course, is an excellent standby, especially if you mix it with a bit of skimmed milk powder. The powder will add richness, as well as an extra dose of calcium, protein and – very important – vitamins A and D.

Hard Cheeses

Most hard cheeses are very fatty, but there are no skimmed milk hard cheeses available yet. Choose medium-fat hard cheeses and use them sparingly. Italian Parmesan is one of the best of the medium-fat cheeses. It has a deep taste, so a little goes a long way. To grate it, put pieces of Parmesan into the blender and blend to a powder. Store in the fridge or freezer. There is now available a ready-grated Italian Parmesan made with vegetarian rennet; it is worth seeking out from your supermarket or cheesemonger. While you are at it, check out other medium-fat, vegetarian rennet cheeses to see which you like. Use them grated, sparingly, in recipes that call for cheese.

Ricotta Cheese

Cream, soured cream and creamy cheeses (such as Italian Mascarpone) hover on the 80 per cent fat range. Ricotta cheese, at 15 per cent fat (or

8 per cent for the lower-fat variety) is an excellent substitute. Strictly speaking, ricotta is not a cheese at all because it is made from whey. It is beautifully creamy and has an exquisite sweetness. Use it by the spoonful in sauces that would normally be made from cream or soured cream. It is available in small pots (15 per cent fat) in the supermarket, and in vacuum packs (8 per cent fat) in Italian delicatessens and speciality shops. Much of the readily available ricotta is suitable for vegetarians.

Italian-Style Mozzarella Cheese

The Italian-style variety, in liquid-filled pouches, now comes in a half-fat (10 per cent fat) version. If you can't find it, even the whole milk version has relatively modest levels (hovering on the 20 per cent fat range), making it very useful (in moderation) for cooking. Mozzarella is a bland, creamy, mild cheese, perfect for melting on pizzas, in lasagne-type dishes, and other Italian delights.

Butter and Margarine

These are virtually pure fat; why not give them up entirely? You certainly don't need them for cooking: this book is filled with techniques that will enable you to cook happily and successfully without them. As for spreading them on bread, good bread is marvellous on its own, so why spoil it with a layer of grease? If you want a spread, use yeast extract, mashed fruit, a little bit of jam, marmalade or honey, or fromage frais or quark flavoured with herbs, spices, honey or marmalade. There is an entire chapter of spreads in this book (see page 34) just crying out for sympathetic slices of bread. As far as 'low-fat spreads' are concerned, they may be *lower* in fat than conventional spreads, but they are still *fat*. Although diluted somewhat with water, buttermilk or what-have-you, they are still, as fat, programmed to go directly to your fat stores with heart-breaking accuracy.

Oils

For many people, oils (especially olive oil) are very hard to give up. Just remember, whatever the oil, it contains 120 calories per tablespoon, and – over a day's eating – those tablespoons add up. It is easier than you think to cook (and to cook well) without lashings of oil. Here are a few tried and tested tricks:

No-Fat Sauté Methods

Sauté (pan-fry) in vegetable stock or a mixture of vegetable stock and wine instead of in butter, margarine or oil. Onions and garlic – the basis of many savoury recipes – work very well sautéed in this way. If you crave the taste of olive oil, instead of reaching for the oil bottle, go directly to the source: good black olives. Choose black olives packed in brine (or dry-packed), and sliver the flesh off the stones into the pan with the onions, garlic and stock. Two black olives will add 7 Calories to a dish (compared to 120 Calories from a single tablespoon of olive oil) and the flavour is lovely. Add an extra punch of flavour by adding two chopped dry-packed sun-dried tomatoes to the stock. Bags of sun-dried tomatoes are now available in many supermarkets, as well as wholefood shops and speciality food stores.

Pan-sautéed mushrooms need no oil or butter either: sauté them instead in a mixture of sherry, Teriyaki or soy sauce, and stock. These three ingredients enhance the natural mushroom flavour in a remarkable way.

Oil and Water Spray

There are times when a few drops of oil ease things along: a baking dish needs to be greased, a frying pan needs oiling, and so on. For such occasions, make yourself an oil and water misting spray. Buy a small plastic spray atomiser bottle (available from the cosmetic or perfume section of many department stores) and fill it seven-eighths full with water, and one-eighth with good olive oil. When you need to oil a pan or lightly oil vegetables for grilling, *shake the bottle* first, then spray lightly. This shake and spritz method will give you a very light misting of water and oil – the water will evaporate in the cooking, leaving a bare minimum of oil that works beautifully. Aim for the lightest water/oil mist, *not* an oily stream. The secret is in the proportions – seven-eighths water and one-eighth oil – and in the technique – always *shake* and *spritz*. You might keep one spray bottle for olive oil and water, and another for rapeseed or sunflower oil and water, for those times when you don't want an olive oil flavour.

Oven-Frying

Throw away your deep-frier and invest in a good non-stick baking sheet (no big investment really; they are not expensive). With the shake and spritz method and the baking sheet, you need never again drown potato pieces in boiling oil. Home-made oven chips are a revelation (see pages 174 and 175 for examples).

The above methods are just as easy as higher-fat conventional cooking methods. Once you get the hang of them, they will become second nature, and low-fat cooking will be no more arduous than any other kind. Very low-fat dishes can be insipid and monotonous; this is one of the reasons so many people have trouble sticking to such a regime. My techniques ensure that this does not happen. If anything, the flavours of foods cooked by these methods are *more* intense than their conventionally made counterparts. Without the blunting effect of fat, all sorts of magnificent flavours shine through.

Other High-Fat Ingredients

There is an erroneous belief that a vegetarian diet is, by definition, a low-fat one, but this is not true. Not only do oils, butter, whole milk and whole-milk products pile on the fat, but there are other high-fat pitfalls to watch out for, such as:

Avocados

In Mexico, they call avocados 'poor man's butter', and spread the unctuous pale green flesh on bread. One avocado (about 10 oz/275 g) contains 320 calories, about 280 of which are fat calories.

Nuts

All types are astronomically high in fat: for instance 1 oz (25 g) almonds (about 24) contains 170 Calories, 140 of which are fat calories, and 1 oz (25 g) peanuts (only 3 tablespoons of the wretched things) contains 160 Calories, 130 of them fat calories.

Coconut

This is high in fat as well; in fact chestnuts are the only nuts that are not. Chestnuts, bless them, contain less than one gram of fat per 1 oz (25 g). All other nuts, alas, derive most of their calories from fat.

Salad Dressings

Obviously, these are extremely high in fat, and *mayonnaise* is virtually pure fat. Dress your salads instead with lemon or lime juice; very low-fat fromage frais mixed with balsamic vinegar and a dab of Dijon mustard; or just plain balsamic vinegar or sherry wine vinegar.

A Low-Fat Diet, not a No-Fat Diet

A totally fat-free diet would be very difficult to achieve, and dangerous as well. A small amount (around 3–4 grams a day) of essential fatty acids is necessary to maintain health, as are the so-called 'fat-soluble' vitamins A, D, and E, that are usually found in the fatty substances of our diet. Cutting out *added* fat, however, should not be a worry. Whole grains are a rich source of essential fatty acids and vitamin E; and green, yellow and orange vegetables are a rich source of carotene (from which our bodies manufacture vitamin A). Skimmed milk powder is fortified with vitamin D, and our bodies can manufacture vitamin D when there is sunlight. Eat a varied diet rich in vegetables and wholegrains, get some sunlight on your arms and face when possible (no need to sunbathe compulsively – just don't cover up too completely on sunny days, and don't stay exclusively indoors) and the absence of *added* fat shouldn't be a problem.

Very Low-Fat Note

If you have been told by your doctor to reduce your dietary fat levels *drastically* then omit these ingredients from the recipes in this book: oil and water spray (see page 5); any medium-fat cheeses (see pages 3–4); tofu; olives. But do make sure you eat a generous amount and wide variety of grains, vegetables, beans, pulses, skimmed milk dairy products, and so on.

The Store Cupboard

With a well stocked freezer, cupboard and vegetable rack, a good meal is always only minutes away. A rack full of garlic, onions and potatoes, a shelf devoted to grains and pasta, a collection of ground spices and dried herbs are just the beginning. Explore the grocery shelves for the best of the convenience foods and stock up.

Canned and Frozen Foods

Canned beans and other pulses, peeled red peppers (pimentos), sweetcorn kernels and tomatoes are store-cupboard staples that make the life of a vegetarian cook much easier. The freezer yields valuable ingredients as well: frozen sweetcorn, garden peas, spinach and filo pastry are excellent products.

Stock

Low-fat vegetable stocks are easier than ever to find: many supermarkets now carry little tubs of ready-made stock on their chill shelves. The stocks are unseasoned, so when you cook them down in a sauté they do not make the finished dish too salty. They can be stored in your freezer in their tubs. Even more convenient (and less expensive) are vegetable bouillon powders. There are two excellent choices available in some wholefood shops: Frigg's Végétal (no fat at all) and Marigold Vegan Bouillon powder (less than one gram of fat per teaspoon). For the stock-sauté method (see page 5), pour water into the frying pan, sprinkle on a little bit of bouillon powder, and you're ready to go. A member of the audience at one of my demonstrations called this the 'fish food' method, because it looks just like you are sprinkling fish food into a fish tank!

Wine

Dry red wine, dry white vermouth and sherry are important components of a low-fat cookery regime. Onions and garlic sautéed in stock and wine make a rich-tasting base on which to build any number of recipes. Mushrooms sautéed in the 'trinity' of low-fat mushroom cookery, stock, sherry and Teriyaki sauce, surpass butter-swamped mushrooms. Brisk simmering eliminates the alcohol so you are left with the flavour, but *not* the alcohol calories. An opened bottle of vermouth or sherry will keep for weeks in a cool corner of your kitchen, so you will not waste the bottle (or feel that you have to drink up the remainder!) after you've used a little in a recipe. An opened bottle of red wine, however, is perishable. A little vacuum pump, designed to pump the air out of the opened bottle, is a handy gadget to own, and will allow you to use what you need and save the remainder.

Bottled Condiments

More and more bottled condiments appear on grocery shelves every day. Look for Hoisin sauce (a sort of Chinese barbecue sauce), Tabasco (hot pepper sauce), Teriyaki sauce (a slightly sweetened soy sauce), spicy ketchup (salsa ketchup, for example), capers and Dijon mustard. A dash or spoonful here and there livens up all sorts of dishes.

Seasonings

Along with the usual salt, pepper and dried herbs and spices, find a good brand of paprika (Hungarian sweet pepper powder) and garam masala (a relatively gentle mix of fragrant curry spices), and keep them on hand. Sun-dried tomatoes add deep but unobtrusive flavour to low-fat dishes: buy the kind that come dry-packed in cellophane pouches as opposed to those that come drowned in oil. Chop up one or two with scissors, and use as a seasoning along with slivered black olives. Niçoise black olives and Greek black olives bottled in brine are just right.

Before You Begin

Following a Recipe

1. Read each recipe through so you know what you need and what you are doing.
2. Gather all the ingredients together and arrange them on your work surface. If you are preparing a curry or chilli that calls for a spice mixture, measure out all the spices into a small bowl. Scrub, peel, and chop all the vegetables, as necessary. Prepare everything so that it is ready to go. The more organised you are, the faster you will be able to cook, and the more you will enjoy it. It is a shame to miss out on the fun of cooking (and eating) because preparations just seem too daunting.
3. All quantities are given in Imperial measurements and in the approximate metric equivalent. Follow one or the other – don't mix them.

Eggs

All eggs used are size 1.

Vegan Recipes

Recipes with a ❤ symbol are suitable for vegans. Where a simple variation to a recipe will make it suitable for vegans, I have indicated this at the end of the recipe.

Freezing

Recipes suitable for freezing are marked with a ⚡ symbol.

A Note on Serving Sizes

The number of people a recipe will serve depends on the way it will be used (many are suitable for serving in several ways: as a starter, a main dish, a side dish and as part of a complement of dishes) and on the appetites of those who will eat it. Whenever possible, I have given the yield in volume rather than numbers of servings, so that you can visualise the amount the recipe makes, and then use it as you wish.

In many cases, it pays to make more than you need, then to freeze or refrigerate the remainder for another day. Leftovers are so versatile. They can be reheated and eaten as they are, or they can be turned into a soup or a sauce, a frittata (flat omelette) filling, or a filling for filo pastry or vegetable cases. There is nothing quite so stimulating as a cache of yesterday's food, just waiting to be transformed into something new and exciting. Of course, in some food-enthusiastic households, there never are any leftovers. If this applies to yours, put anything you want to save into an opaque-lidded container, label it 'tripe in prune sauce', and tuck it away at the back of the fridge!

Non-Reactive Cookware

Cast-iron, tin and aluminium cookware will react with acid ingredients, such as tomatoes, wine and spinach, to produce off-flavours and discolorations. To avoid these problems, use *non-reactive* cookware, such as enamelled cast iron, stainless steel or flame-proof glass, or cookware with a non-stick coating.

Soups

The soups in this chapter overflow with comfort and big, round
flavour. A large bowlful (or two), with a crusty loaf of wholemeal
bread, makes a gutsy meal that needs no other embellishment. The no-
fat techniques ensure full flavour despite the lack of butter, oil or cream:
'cream' soups are made creamy with rich purées of vegetables; soups
based on sautéed vegetables are built on stock-sautéed vegetables that
have been infused with herbs and spices, sun-dried tomatoes and
(occasionally) a few olives. Robust fresh flavours shine through with no
muffling fat to get in the way.

SERVING NOTE

In very general terms, ½ pint (300 ml) soup is enough for a starter for
one person, 1 pint (600 ml) is enough for a main course. Do feel free to
adjust this to the appetites of those who will eat the soups.

Lentil Soup

· · · · · · · · · · · · **V** · **Z** · · · · · · · · · · ·

Makes 2 ¹/₂ pints (1.4 litres)

If lentils are soaked ahead of time, their cooking time is shortened, and they need less liquid. However, I always find it easier just to throw the unsoaked lentils in, give them as much liquid as they need, and allow them to simmer quietly until ready. Don't add salt early in the cooking, and use bottled water if your water is very hard, or the lentils may never become tender.

3½ pints (2 litres) salt-free stock or water

4 fl oz (100 ml) dry red wine

1 large mild onion, chopped

2 garlic cloves, crushed

3 dry-packed sun-dried tomatoes, chopped (use scissors)

8 oz (225 g) brown or green lentils, rinsed and picked over

14 oz (400 g) can of chopped tomatoes

vegetable bouillon powder (optional)

salt and freshly ground pepper

1 Combine ½ pint (300 ml) of the stock or water, the wine, onion, garlic and sun-dried tomatoes in a heavy-bottomed saucepan. Cover, bring to the boil, and boil for 5–7 minutes. Uncover, reduce the heat, and simmer until the onions are tender and the liquid almost gone.

2 Stir in the lentils, remaining stock or water, and tomatoes. Simmer, partially covered, for 45–60 minutes or until the lentils are very tender. If you have used water, you can stir in some vegetable bouillon powder when the lentils are tender. In either case, season with salt and pepper.

3 Ladle a quarter to a third of the soup into a blender, and purée in small batches. Stir the purée back into the soup and reheat gently before serving.

Black Bean Soup

· · · · · · · · · · · · · ✦ · · · · · · · · · · · · · ·

Makes 3 1/2 pints (2 litres)

*Black beans (sometimes referred to as turtle beans) are purply-black
kidney beans, and a staple in Spanish, Cuban and Mexican cookery.
The soaked and cooked beans make a suave and subtle purée, used to
advantage in many classic soups. This recipe combines traditions of
Spain and Mexico.*

2 1/2 pints (1.4 litres) soaked and
   cooked black beans (see page
   111)
2 pints (1.1 litres) stock
juice and slivered zest of 1 small
   orange
1/4 pint (150 ml) dry sherry
salt and freshly ground black
   pepper

TO SERVE
cooked rice (optional)
fromage frais
1 orange, peeled and thinly sliced
fresh coriander leaves

1 Combine the beans, stock and orange zest in a saucepan. Bring to
the boil, then reduce the heat and simmer for 30 minutes. Cool slightly.

2 Purée the soup in a blender in small batches, then push the purée
through a sieve into a clean saucepan.

3 Pour in the sherry and orange juice, and simmer for 10 minutes.
Taste and adjust the seasoning.

4 If you are using the rice, put a spoonful in the bottom of each
warmed soup bowl, and fill with soup. Put a spoonful of fromage frais
on the surface, and lay an orange slice on each side. Sprinkle with
coriander leaves.

V Omit the fromage frais

Chestnut Soup

. . . .

Makes 2¹/₂ pints (1.4 litres)

Red wine, bay leaf and chestnuts have a natural affinity for each other, and come together very well in this festive soup. It would make the perfect beginning to a Christmas dinner.

6 shallots, chopped
12 oz (350 g) carrots, chopped
1 large celery stalk, chopped
3 pints (2 litres) stock
6 fl oz (175 ml) dry red wine
three 12 oz (350 g) cans of
  unsweetened chestnuts,
  drained

1 bay leaf
¹/₄ teaspoon freshly grated
  nutmeg
salt and freshly ground pepper
2 tablespoons skimmed milk
  powder
8 fl oz (225 ml) skimmed milk

1 Put the shallots, carrots and celery in a large saucepan. Add 4 fl oz (100 ml) of the stock and 2 fl oz (50 ml) of the wine, cover and bring to the boil. Boil until almost all the liquid has cooked away.

2 Add the chestnuts, remaining stock, the bay leaf, nutmeg, and salt and pepper to taste. Simmer, partially covered, for 20–30 minutes, then cool slightly and remove the bay leaf.

3 Purée the soup in small batches in a blender, then return it to the saucepan. Mix the milk and skimmed milk powder, and stir into the soup. Bring back to a simmer and simmer for 10 minutes. If serving at once, stir in the remaining wine, and simmer, uncovered for 5–10 minutes, before pouring into warmed soup bowls.

4 If not serving at once, cool and refrigerate before adding the remaining wine. At serving time, bring to a simmer, stir in the remaining wine and simmer, uncovered, for 5–10 minutes.

Creamy Parsnip Soup

· · · · · · · · · · · · · · **V** · **Z** · · · · · · · · · · · · · ·

Makes 2¹/₄ pints (1.3 litres)

Curried parsnip soup, laced with lashings of butter and cream, has become a British classic. I find parsnip purée enticingly rich, and creamy enough without the fatty butter/cream dimension. Adding a potato gives body, and garam masala gives a subtler spiciness than does curry powder. Like many of the soups in this chapter, creamy parsnip soup is a deeply soothing brew.

I large mild onion, chopped
¹/₂ inch (I cm) piece of fresh root ginger, peeled and crushed
2 garlic cloves, crushed
3 pints (I.7 litres) stock
I teaspoon garam masala

I lb (450 g) parsnips, diced
I medium all-purpose (e.g. Wilja) potato, scrubbed and coarsely diced
salt and freshly ground pepper

I Put the onion, ginger, garlic and ¹/₂ pint (300 ml) stock in a heavy-bottomed saucepan, cover and bring to the boil. Boil for 5–7 minutes, then uncover, reduce the heat slightly and simmer, stirring, until the onions are tender and the liquid almost gone. Add the garam masala and stir so that the onions are well coated with the spices.

2 Stir in the parsnips, potato and remaining stock. Simmer for 10–15 minutes or until the parsnips and potatoes are very tender. Season with salt and pepper, then leave to cool slightly.

3 Purée the soup in batches in a blender until smooth and velvety. Return the soup to the pan and heat gently. Check the seasonings, and serve.

Puréed Vegetable–Bean Soup

· · · · · · · · · · · · · · ⓥ · · ⓩ · · · · · · · · · · · · · ·

Makes 3¹/₂ pints (2 litres)

The crunch of croûtons against the velvety smoothness of the vegetable–bean purée gives a little touch of gastronomic heaven. The garlic in the soup is mellow and mild because it has been simmered in stock; the garlic on the croûtons is strong because it has been rubbed on rude and raw. If you'd rather skip the rudeness, prepare the croûtons without the garlic rub. The crunch–velvet contrast of croûton–soup will still send frissons of pleasure up and down your spine.

2 garlic cloves, crushed

1 medium onion, diced

2–3 black olives in brine, drained and flesh slivered off the stones

¹/₄ teaspoon crushed dried chillies (or to taste)

2¹/₂ pints (1.4 litres) stock

2 lb (900 g) mixed vegetables, coarsely chopped: courgettes, small white turnips, carrots, all-purpose potatoes (e.g. Wilja), green peas (frozen are fine)

salt and freshly ground pepper

2 tablespoons shredded fresh basil

1 tablespoon chopped fresh parsley

15 oz (432 g) can cannellini beans, drained and rinsed

Garlic Croûtons (see box), to serve

1 Put the garlic, onion, olive pieces, chillies and ¹/₂ pint (300 ml) stock in a heavy-bottomed saucepan, cover and bring to the boil. Boil for 5 minutes, then reduce the heat slightly, uncover and simmer until the onion is tender and the liquid almost gone.

2 Add all the vegetables (except the cannellini beans), and season with salt and pepper. Cook gently, stirring, for a few minutes, then stir in the remaining stock. Simmer, covered, for 30–35 minutes, then stir in the herbs and beans, and cook for a few minutes more or until all the vegetables are tender. Leave to cool slightly.

3 Purée the soup in small batches in a blender until very smooth. Taste and adjust the seasonings, and serve sprinkled with croûtons.

GARLIC CROÛTONS

Dry slices of day-old bread in the oven at 350°F, 180°C, Gas Mark 4, turning occasionally. When they are dry and crisp right through, remove them from the oven, and rub each slice thoroughly with the cut side of a garlic clove. Cut or break the slices into rough $^1/_4$–$^1/_2$ inch (0.5–1 cm) cubes.

Squash Soup in a Squash

Serves 1

Acorn squash is one of the 'winter squashes'; sturdy, gourd-like vegetables available in supermarkets during the autumn and winter months. When baked, the inner flesh becomes ineffably sweet and tender, but the shell holds its shape. In this recipe, acorn squash becomes a mini-tureen, holding a gentle brew of stock and cheese, making this a most dramatic – and most comforting – soup. This makes one serving; multiply it to make as many as you need.

1 acorn squash
2 spring onions, trimmed and sliced
1 garlic clove, crushed
about ½ pint (300 ml) hot stock

1 tablespoon breadcrumbs
salt and freshly ground pepper
pinch of freshly grated nutmeg
1 tablespoon grated Parmesan (or other medium-fat cheese)

1 Preheat the oven to 400°F, 200°C, Gas Mark 8.

2 If necessary, cut a very thin slice off the bottom of the squash so that it sits on a level bottom. Be careful – there must be no leaks in the squash, and the bottom must remain thick. Cut a 'cap' off the top of the squash and scrape out the seeds and fibres.

3 Put the onions and garlic in a saucepan with a little of the stock, and simmer until the onions are tender and the liquid gone. Add the breadcrumbs, and stir until the onions and crumbs are well combined. Remove from heat, season with salt and pepper, and stir in the nutmeg and cheese.

4 Spoon the crumb–cheese mixture into the squash. Pour in enough of the remaining stock to fill the squash seven-eighths full, and place the 'cap' back on the squash.

5 Put the squash in a non-stick baking dish and bake in the oven for 45 minutes to 1 hour or until the soup is simmering and the inside of the squash is becoming tender.

6 Reduce the oven temperature to 300°F, 150°C, Gas Mark 2, and continue to bake for a further 15–20 minutes or until the inside of the squash is quite tender. Remember, the outside of the squash must not lose its shape.

7 Taste the soup, adjust the seasonings, and serve the squash, set in a soup bowl, at once. To eat, spoon out the soup along with the tender squash flesh.

Green Velvet Soup

· · · · · · · · · · · · · · · ❍ · ❍ · · · · · · · · · · · · · ·

Makes 3 pints (1.7 litres)

This is another velvet-textured soup that cries out for the crunch of croûtons (see page 17). This may sound very odd, but if you want instant no-fat croûtons, try bite-sized Shredded Wheat; they are brilliant as a soup garnish. A handful of freshly popped popcorn (see box) will happily garnish a bowl of creamy soup as well.

I large mild onion, coarsely chopped

4 celery stalks, coarsely chopped

2 garlic cloves, crushed

¼ small green or white cabbage, cored and coarsely chopped

I small head of fennel, coarsely chopped

3 small courgettes, coarsely diced

8–9 oz (225–250 g) bunch broccoli, coarsely chopped

4 oz (100 g) runner beans, sliced into I inch (2.5 cm) pieces

I medium all-purpose (e.g. Wilja) potato, scrubbed and coarsely diced

2 pints (1.1 litres) stock

salt and freshly ground pepper

6 tablespoons chopped fresh parsley

4 tablespoons shredded fresh basil

1 Combine all the ingredients, except the herbs, in a large, heavy-bottomed saucepan. Cover and bring to the boil, then reduce the heat and simmer partially covered, for 45 minutes, stirring occasionally. Add the herbs and more salt and pepper, if necessary. Simmer for 5–10 minutes more, then leave to cool slightly.

2 Purée the soup in small batches in a blender until *very* smooth and velvety, then push through a sieve back into a saucepan. Reheat, taste and adjust the seasonings before serving.

MICROWAVE POPCORN

Makes 3¹/₂ pints (2 litres)

Store corn for popping in the freezer and cook from frozen – the popcorn will be exceptionally fluffy. Microwave ovens are not consistent, so you will have to check the time given in this recipe by testing it in your particular machine. If the popcorn stays in too long, it scorches. Do not buy 'microwave popcorn' as it contains added fat. Just buy plain, unadorned popcorn.

1 Pour the popping corn into a 3¹/₂ pint (2 litre), 9 inch (23 cm) diameter microwave-proof glass bowl. Put in just enough to make a single layer, patting it down so that it covers the bottom of the dish evenly. Cover tightly with microwave cling film.

2 Microwave on high (100%) for 3–7 minutes.

3 Pierce the cling film to release the steam (avert your face), then carefully peel off the cling film and tip the popcorn into a bowl.

Creamy and Spicy Potato Soup

· · · · · · · · · · · · · · ·**V**· ·**Z**· · · · · · · · · ·

Makes 4 pints (2.3 litres)

This is a magnificent soup to make in quantity, and then freeze in individual portions, although you and your housemates might easily polish off a whole batch in a day or two. Although an entire head of garlic is used, it gives textural substance and flavour without harsh vulgarity. The colour, a glowing apricot, is lovely as well. If you have no grilled peppers on hand for the garnish (see page 131), canned or bottled red peppers (pimentos) can be puréed and seasoned instead.

1½ tablespoons sesame seeds

1 tablespoon fennel seeds

1 teaspoon cumin seeds

1 head of garlic

3 medium onions, halved and sliced into thin half moons

2½ pints (1.4 litres) stock

6 medium (about 1¾ lb/800 g) all-purpose (e.g. Wilja) potatoes, peeled and quartered

salt and freshly ground pepper

1 large red pepper, deseeded and coarsely chopped

1 lb (450 g) sweetcorn kernels

14 oz (400 g) can of chopped Italian tomatoes

1 tablespoon fresh lime juice

GARNISH

Puréed grilled peppers (see page 131) seasoned with a dab of honey (or brown sugar for vegans) and a dash of Tabasco sauce

1 Put all the seeds in a heavy-bottomed saucepan, and heat gently for about 1 minute or until lightly toasted and fragrant, stirring constantly.

2 Separate the head of garlic into cloves. Hit each clove lightly with a kitchen mallet or the flat side of a wide-bladed knife to loosen the skin, then remove and discard the skin.

3 Put the onions and garlic into the saucepan with the seeds. Pour in ½ pint (300 ml) stock, cover and bring to the boil, then reduce the heat and simmer briskly for 5 minutes. Uncover and continue to cook over moderate heat, stirring occasionally, for 5–10 minutes or until the onions are tender and the stock has almost cooked away.

4 Add the potatoes, stir and cook for 2–3 minutes more.

5 Stir in the remaining ingredients except the garnish, and simmer, partially covered, for 30 minutes or until the potatoes are very tender. Skim off the foam occasionally as it cooks. Leave to cool slightly.

6 Purée the mixture in small batches in a blender, then push it through a sieve. To serve reheat the soup and adjust the seasonings, then pour into warmed soup bowls, and garnish with a swirl of puréed grilled peppers seasoned with a little honey or brown sugar and a dash of Tabasco sauce.

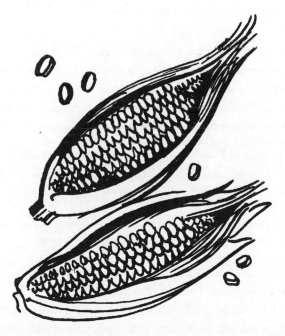

Simple Vegetable Soup

· · · · · · · · · · · · · · · **V** · · **Z** · · · · · · · · · · · · · ·

Makes 2¹/₂ pints (1.4 litres)

This recipe demonstrates how good the stock–sauté method (see page 5) can be: the fresh vegetable flavour, unhampered by any fat, just shines through.

2 medium carrots, coarsely diced

1 large onion, halved and sliced into thin half moons

3 garlic cloves, crushed

2¹/₂ pints (1.4 litres) stock

3 peppers (1 red, 1 yellow, 1 green), peeled, deseeded and coarsely diced

3 small courgettes, coarsely diced

5 ripe tomatoes, peeled, deseeded and quartered (substitute canned tomatoes when good tomatoes are unavailable)

salt and freshly ground pepper

3 tablespoons chopped fresh parsley

1 bunch of chives, finely snipped

1 Put the carrots, onion, garlic and ¹/₂ pint (300 ml) stock in a heavy-bottomed saucepan. Cover, bring to the boil, and boil for 7 minutes. Uncover, reduce the heat slightly and simmer briskly until the onions and carrots are tender and the liquid almost gone. Add the peppers and a splash of stock, and cook, stirring, for a few minutes more.

2 Stir in the courgettes, tomatoes and remaining stock, and simmer for 10–15 minutes or until everything is tender. Season with salt and pepper, and stir in the herbs. Cook for 1–2 minutes more.

PRESSING MATTERS

Be kind to garlic, and don't subject it to a garlic press, which turns it into an acrid mess. Instead, buy a wooden mallet at a DIY shop and use it to crush garlic cloves: hit each clove lightly with the mallet to loosen the skin, then remove the skin and crush the clove with the mallet. This down-to-earth wooden implement also works well crushing slices of fresh ginger root. Alternatively, use the bottom of a bottle or the flat side of a wide knife.

Colourful Corn Chowder

· · · · · · · · · · · · · · **Z** · · · · · · · · · · · · · ·

Makes 3 pints (1.7 litres)

This chowder bursts with colour, texture and nutrition, and, served with a crusty loaf of bread, would make a splendid evening meal. Frozen corn (especially the corn that has been cultivated for extra sweetness) is better than the 'fresh' corn you can buy in the supermarket. It pays to keep some in the freezer.

12 spring onions, sliced

2–3 dry-packed sun-dried tomatoes, chopped (use scissors)

2 carrots, coarsely chopped

1 large red pepper, peeled, deseeded and coarsely chopped

1 fresh chilli, deseeded and finely chopped

1–2 garlic cloves, crushed

1/2 teaspoon ground cumin

1/2 teaspoon ground coriander

2 pints (1.1 litres) stock

8 oz (225 g) all-purpose (e.g. Wilja) potatoes, cut into 1/2 inch (1 cm) cubes

1 lb (450 g) frozen sweetcorn kernels

salt and freshly ground pepper

8 fl oz (225 ml) skimmed milk

2 tablespoons skimmed milk powder

3–4 tablespoons chopped fresh coriander

3–4 tablespoons shredded fresh mint

1 Put the onions, tomatoes, carrots, red pepper, chilli, garlic and spices in a large heavy-bottomed sauce with 1/2 pint (300 ml) stock. Cover, bring to the boil and boil for 3–5 minutes. Stir in the potatoes and simmer for 3–4 minutes more, until the liquid has almost gone.

2 Stir in the remaining stock, and simmer, partially covered, for about 5 minutes or until the potatoes are almost tender. Stir in the corn, season with salt and pepper and simmer until all the vegetables are tender. Remove from the heat.

3 Mix the milk and skimmed milk powder and stir into the soup. Ladle out 1/2 pint (300 ml) of the soup and purée it in small batches in a blender until smooth. Stir the purée back into the saucepan, taste and adjust the seasonings.

4 Simmer for 3–4 minutes, then stir in the herbs before serving.

Mushroom Barley Soup

· · · · · · · · · · ⓥ · ⓩ · · · · · · · · · ·

Makes 6 halves

Mushroom Barley Soup is a beloved and enduring Russian/Jewish classic. The real thing contains a frightening amount of rendered chicken fat; double anathema for low-fat vegetarians. By any standard, substituting the non-fat mushroom sauté method for the chicken fat improves the classic immeasurably. Pot barley (available in wholefood shops) has had less processing than pearl barley (available in supermarkets), and therefore contains more nutrients. It is worth seeking out the pot variety: it will take longer to cook than the pearl variety, and will be chewier (this is actually a plus – the texture is wonderful). If you choose to use the easier-to-find pearl barley, cut about 15 minutes off the cooking time.

1 oz (25 g) dried *porcini* mushrooms
³/₄ pint (450 ml) hot water
1¹/₂ lb (700 g) fresh mushrooms (preferably brown cap), cut into quarters or eighths, depending on size
2 garlic cloves, crushed

8 spring onions, sliced
4 fl oz (100 ml) dry sherry
several dashes of Teriyaki or soy sauce
2 pints (1.1 litres) stock
4 oz (100 g) pot barley, rinsed
salt and freshly ground pepper

1 Rinse the dried mushrooms well under cold running water. Put them in a bowl with the hot water and leave to soak for 20–30 minutes.

2 Put the fresh mushrooms, garlic, spring onions, sherry and Teriyaki or soy sauce in a heavy-bottomed saucepan. Cook, stirring occasionally, until the mushrooms begin to exude a great deal of liquid and to turn dark.

3 Strain the soaking water from the dried mushrooms through a sieve lined with a double layer of muslin or coffee filter papers, and reserve mushrooms and soaking water. Rinse the soaked mushrooms under cold running water, and trim off and discard any tough stems. Cut the mushrooms into coarse pieces. Add them to the soup along with their strained soaking water. Add the stock and barley, season with salt and pepper, and simmer, partially covered, for 1 hour or until the barley is tender. Taste and adjust the seasoning.

DRIED MUSHROOMS

Dried *Boletus edulis* mushrooms (*porcini* in Italian, *cèpes* in French) are available in 1/2 or 1 oz (15 or 25 g) packages in speciality food shops and some supermarkets. You need no more than 1 oz (25 g): when reconstituted they plump up to about five times their dried weight, and the flavour will be up to twenty times as intense as that of 1 oz (25 g) of the same mushrooms in their undried (fresh) state. They must be rinsed well before soaking, and after soaking their powerfully flavoured soaking water should be strained to eliminate the copious sand that lurks in their nooks and crannies.

Red Pepper Soup

· · · · · · · · · · · · · · V · Z · · · · · · · · · · · · · ·

Makes 3 pints (1.7 litres)

I can't keep my hands off red peppers; the colour, the flavour, the luscious texture of the peppers when they have been divested of their skins, sautéed in stock and puréed . . . For this soup, I've used both smoky grilled peppers, and raw peppers that have been peeled with a swivel-bladed peeler. They combine beautifully with paprika (a close relative) to make a glowing, restorative soup. Bottled or canned red peppers (pimentos) could be used instead of the grilled peppers.

8 large red peppers
1 large mild onion, chopped
1 garlic clove, crushed
1 tablespoon paprika
2½ pints (1.4 litres) stock

1 medium (6–8 oz/175–225 g) all-purpose (e.g Wilja) potato, peeled and coarsely diced
salt and freshly ground pepper

1 Grill and peel three of the peppers (see page 131), then deseed and coarsely dice them. Peel the remaining five peppers with a swivel-bladed peeler (see box), then deseed and coarsely dice them.

2 Put the onion, garlic and paprika in a heavy-bottomed saucepan with ½ pint (300 ml) of the stock. Cover, bring to the boil, and boil for 4–5 minutes, then uncover, reduce the heat and simmer until the onions are tender and are gently 'frying' in their own juices.

3 Stir in the chopped raw peppers with a further ½ pint (300 ml) stock. Simmer for a few minutes, stirring occasionally, until the peppers begin to soften, then stir in the potato and cook for 2–3 minutes more.

4 Stir in the remaining stock and the grilled peppers, and season with salt and pepper. Simmer, partially covered, for about 30 minutes or until the vegetables are very tender. Leave to cool slightly.

5 Purée half the soup in small batches in a blender until smooth. Combine the puréed and unpuréed portions, reheat gently, taste and adjust the seasonings.

PEPPERS

Red and yellow peppers are the jewels of vegetarian cookery. One or two of them will add a blaze of colour to a stew or casserole, or several of them can be used to make a rich sauce or soup. Peel raw peppers with a swivel-bladed peeler. It's not unlike peeling a carrot or potato, except first, for ease of peeling, the pepper should be cut into its natural sections. The skin of peppers is not very digestible – peeling them makes then intestinely acceptable to many people who would, normally, avoid them. Also, the cooked pepper pieces are so much more supple and tasty if they have been peeled first. And when peeled peppers are sautéed no-fat style, in stock, their juices form a delicious, syrupy sauce.

Celeriac, Cauliflower and Bean Soup with Fennel Seeds

· · · · · · · · · · · · · · **V** · **Z** · · · · · · · · · · · · · ·

Makes 2 ¹/₂ pints (1.4 litres)

Celeriac is a big, ungainly root (something like a swede in appearance) with a pleasing, starchy character, and a celery-like flavour. Although only half a root is used in this soup, it pays to steam or roast the entire root, or the cut side of the uncooked half will discolour. And there is so much that you can do with a hunk of cooked celeriac. Best of all is to purée it and combine it with mashed potatoes. See the section on foil-roasted vegetables (see page 136) for more ideas.

1 teaspoon fennel seeds

2–3 dry-packed sun-dried tomatoes, chopped (use scissors)

1–2 garlic cloves, crushed

6 spring onions, sliced

pinch of crushed dried chillies (or to taste)

2 black olives in brine, drained and flesh slivered off the stones

4 fl oz (100 ml) dry red wine

2 pints (1.1 litres) stock

1 small cauliflower, separated into florets and steamed

¹/₂ peeled, cooked celeriac root (either steamed or roasted, see page 140), cubed

3 tablespoons tomato purée

15 oz (432 g) can of pinto or borlotti beans, drained and rinsed

salt and freshly ground pepper

1–2 tablespoons chopped fresh parsley

1 Put the fennel seeds, sun-dried tomatoes, garlic, onions, dried chilli, olive pieces and wine in a large heavy-bottomed saucepan with 4 fl oz (100 ml) of the stock. Cover and bring to the boil, then reduce the heat and simmer for 5–7 minutes or until the garlic and onions are tender and the liquid greatly reduced and syrupy.

2 Add the cauliflower, celeriac and another 3 fl oz (75 ml) stock to the pan. Stir gently to allow the vegetables to soak up the flavourful liquid.

3 Stir the tomato purée into the remaining stock, and add it to the pan with the beans. Season with salt and pepper, and simmer for 5–6 minutes. Stir in the parsley.

Chunky Grilled Pepper Gazpacho with Tomato Sorbet

· · · · · · · · · · · · ❖ · · · · · · · · · · · ·

Makes 3 pints (1.7 litres)

Cold soup is perfect for summer alfresco meals. This bursting-with-summer soup is meant to be served in white china or clear glass (to show off the jewel-like colour), with a single, dramatic scoop of tomato sorbet nestling in the centre of each serving.

two 1³/₄ lb (800 g) cans of Italian tomatoes

4 fresh ripe, flavourful tomatoes, peeled and deseeded

finely chopped fresh chilli, to taste

2 fl oz (50 ml) balsamic vinegar or sherry wine vinegar

1–2 garlic cloves, finely chopped

2 tablespoons chopped fresh parsley

2 tablespoons shredded fresh mint or basil

4 red peppers (or 2 red peppers and 2 yellow peppers), grilled and peeled (see page 131), deseeded and coarsely chopped

Tomato Sorbet (see page 32)

1 Drain the canned tomatoes, reserving the juice. Chop the canned and fresh tomatoes.

2 Mix all the ingredients, including the reserved tomato juice, in a large bowl, and chill thoroughly. Serve in shallow bowls or in goblets, with a small scoop of tomato sorbet in the centre of each serving.

Tomato Sorbet

· · · · · · · · · · · · · · V · · · · · · · · · · · · · ·

Makes 1 pint (600 ml)

frozen tomatoes from two 14 oz (400 g) cans of tomatoes (see note)

juice of 1 lime

4 tablespoons shredded fresh basil or mint

several dashes of Tabasco sauce

1 Put all the ingredients in the bowl of a food processor, and process, stopping to scrape down the sides as necessary, until the mixture forms an icy sorbet consistency.

2 With an ice cream scoop, scoop the icy mixture into balls and serve at once.

NOTE

To freeze canned tomatoes, first drain them very well. Halve the tomatoes, spread them out in one layer on a non-stick baking sheet, and freeze solid. When frozen, gather into a plastic food bag, seal and store in the freezer until needed.

Cold Beetroot Borscht

· · · · · · · · · · · · · · · ✆ · · · · · · · · · · · · · ·

Makes 2 ¹/₂ pints (1.4 litres)

Why are beetroots so under-appreciated? When fresh beetroot is available, try this classic sweet and sour chilled Russian soup. No-fat fromage frais is a perfect substitute for the usual soured cream. If you have a processor with a shredding or grating attachment, then the vegetable preparation will be a snap. It is traditional occasionally to set a steaming hot potato right in the centre of each bowlful of icy soup, for a 'hot as summer, cold as winter' effect.

4 raw beetroots, about 8–10 oz (225–275 g) each, peeled and grated
2 large carrots, grated
14 oz (400 g) can of tomatoes
2 leeks, cleaned and chopped
2¹/₂ pints (1.4 litres) water

2 tablespoons tomato purée
3 tablespoons lemon juice
2 tablespoons sugar
salt
no-fat fromage frais and chopped fresh dill, to serve

1 Put the beetroot, carrot, tomatoes and their juice (break up the tomatoes with your fingers), leeks and water in a heavy-bottomed saucepan. Cover and bring to the boil, then reduce the heat and simmer, partially covered, for 45 minutes.

2 Add the tomato purée, lemon juice and sugar, and season with salt. Simmer for a further few minutes.

Taste and add additional lemon juice, sugar or salt, as necessary. The soup should be tart, but not unpleasantly so.

3 Leave the soup to cool, and then chill. Top each serving with a dollop of fromage frais and a sprinkling of dill.

❤ Omit the fromage frais

Dips and Spreads

Many of the recipes in this chapter can be surrounded by a profusion of colourful raw vegetable crudités, or no-fat crisps and chips (see pages 46–8), and served as a sociable first course or a light lunch. Some make good sandwich spreads and fillings, others work well as garnishes. In fact, you will find these dips and spreads infinitely versatile and suitable for both everyday eating and entertaining.

Mushroom–Apple Pâté

· · · · · · · · · · · · · **V** · · · · · · · · · · · · ·

Makes 1³/₄ pints (1 litre)

This pâté is just right spread on small Motzah crackers or Hi–Lo biscuits, or triangles of toast. Use brown cap mushrooms for a nice, dark colour, and don't blend it too smoothly – a slightly rough texture is much more interesting.

3 oz (75 g) dried apple, cut into
  pieces
8 fl oz (225 ml) dry sherry
4 fl oz (100 ml) water
2 lb (900 g) brown cap
  mushrooms, sliced
1–2 garlic cloves, finely chopped

4 fl oz (100 ml) stock
1–2 dashes of Teriyaki sauce
1 teaspoon ground coriander
1–2 pinches of cayenne pepper
salt and freshly ground pepper

1 Put the apple pieces in a bowl with 4 fl oz (100 ml) of the sherry and the water, and leave to soak.

2 Meanwhile, put the mushrooms, garlic, stock, remaining sherry and Teriyaki sauce in a heavy-bottomed frying pan. Bring to the boil, then reduce the heat and simmer briskly, stirring occasionally, until the liquid has almost gone. Add the apples and their soaking liquid, the coriander and cayenne. Simmer, stirring occasionally, until all the liquid has gone. Season with salt and pepper, and leave to cool slightly.

3 Place the mushroom mixture in a food processor and process to a slightly rough purée. Mound the mixture in a bowl, cover and refrigerate until needed.

Duxelles

· · · · · · · · · · · · · · (V) · (Z) · · · · · · · · · · · · · ·

Makes 1 pint (600 ml)

The classic French method for Duxelles – a sort of mushroom hash – calls for finely chopped mushrooms to be sautéed in butter and oil. Substituting my mushroom sauté method, using stock, sherry and soy or Teriyaki sauce, works like a dream; it concentrates and enhances the flavour of the mushrooms. Duxelles is a very useful mixture – spread it on toast, or use it to fill filo pastry (see pages 193 and 194) or (for a double mushroom whammy) to fill poached or steamed-roasted mushrooms (see pages 49 and 126).

2 lb (900 g) brown cap
   mushrooms
8 fl oz (225 ml) stock
4 fl oz (100 ml) sherry
several dashes of Teriyaki sauce

6 spring onions, chopped
1 teaspoon dried tarragon,
   crumbled
salt and freshly ground pepper

1 Chop the mushrooms very, very finely. This is best done by 'pulsing' roughly chopped mushrooms in a food processor. Quarter the mushrooms and put them in the food processor. 'Pulse' the machine on and off quickly until the mushrooms are very finely chopped. You will need to do this in two or more batches.

2 Empty all the chopped mushrooms into a deep, heavy-bottomed frying pan. Add the stock, sherry, Teriyaki sauce, spring onions and tarragon, and stir well. (The mushrooms will be barely moistened but it doesn't matter.)

3 Cook over moderate heat, stirring occasionally, until the mushrooms have rendered quite a bit of liquid. Increase the heat slightly, and simmer briskly, stirring occasionally, until the mushrooms are very dark, very thick and quite dry. Reduce the heat as the liquid cooks away, to minimise scorching. Season with salt and pepper. Spoon into a bowl, cool, cover and store in the refrigerator until needed.

Green Pea Dip

· · · · · · · · · · V · · · · · · · · · · · · ·

Makes 1 pint (600 ml)

Frozen peas, like frozen sweetcorn, are handy to have in the freezer at all times. If you have a microwave, they can be thawed and ready to go in minutes. Both vegetables take to the freezing process very well indeed. This dip has a vividly fresh character – to call it 'garden-fresh' is to lapse into cliché, but I could hardly describe it any other way, even if it has been harvested from the freezer! I often use this as a kind of substitute Guacamole (Mexican avocado spread). If you want to give it a slightly more Mexican character, add some ground cumin and chopped fresh coriander.

juice of 1 lime
1 fresh chilli pepper, deseeded and chopped
4 tablespoons chopped fresh parsley

1 lb (450 g) thawed frozen peas
3–4 spring onions, chopped
salt

1 Place all the ingredients, except the spring onions and salt, in a blender or food processor, and process until coarsely chopped.

2 Add the onions, season with salt, and process to a rough purée. Spoon into a bowl, cover and refrigerate until required.

Roasted Vegetable Dip

ⓥ

Makes 1 pint (600 ml)

Spread this deeply flavoured purée on bread, scoop it up with vegetable dippers, or, if you can't wait to dive in, eat it with a spoon. It's the roasting (especially of the garlic) and the smokiness of the grilled peppers that give the purée its depth. Roasting garlic in this manner renders the bulb mellow and sweet: one clove of raw garlic, pushed through a garlic press, is actually stronger than an entire roasted bulb.

2 medium aubergines, about 8 oz (225 g) each

1 large, firm head of garlic

2 red peppers, grilled and peeled (see page 131), then diced (or use canned or bottled red peppers or pimentos)

1 large ripe tomato, peeled, deseeded and chopped (or, out of season, use 2–3 canned Italian tomatoes, drained and chopped)

juice of ½ lemon

4 spring onions, cut in half lengthways and sliced across thinly

6 tablespoons chopped fresh parsley

3 tablespoons chopped fresh mint or basil

salt and freshly ground pepper

1 Preheat the oven to 375°F, 190°C, Gas Mark 5.

2 Prick the aubergines in several places with a fork or thin skewer. Remove the papery outer covering of the garlic, but do not separate the cloves. Wrap the garlic in foil. Bake both aubergines and garlic directly on the oven shelf for 45–55 minutes or until the aubergine is soft and collapsed, and the garlic is soft within its skin. Leave to cool on a wire rack.

3 When both the aubergines and garlic are cool enough to handle, trim the stems from the aubergines and strip off the skin. Roughly chop the aubergines and put in a bowl. Separate the garlic cloves, and squeeze each clove over the bowl so that the puréed garlic pops out (in fact, it *oozes* out, just like toothpaste from a tube) into the bowl.

4 Add the remaining ingredients to the bowl. With an electric beater, beat the mixture into a rough purée, or pulse on and off in a food processor. Taste and adjust the seasoning, adding more salt, pepper and lemon juice as needed. Cover and chill for at least 1 hour before serving.

Mellow Garlic and Lentil Spread

· · · · · · · · · · · · · ⓥ · · · · · · · · · · · · ·

Makes 1 pint (600 ml)

Red lentils need no soaking, cook quickly, and can be used to make lovely spreads for bread. Three versions follow; the first features mild garlic, the second has an Italian accent, and the third combines lemon juice with a lively spice mixture.

8 oz (225 g) split red lentils, rinsed

3 garlic cloves, halved

1 pint (600 ml) salt-free stock or water

salt and freshly ground pepper

1–2 dashes of Teriyaki sauce

a few drops of Tabasco sauce

¼ teaspoon Dijon mustard

vegetable bouillon powder (optional)

1 Put the lentils, garlic and stock or water in a heavy-bottomed saucepan. Bring to the boil, then reduce the heat and simmer, uncovered, for 20–30 minutes or until the lentils are tender. Skim off foam from the surface from time to time, and add more liquid if needed to prevent scorching.

2 Season the mixture with the remaining ingredients (adding some vegetable bouillon powder if you have used water instead of salt-free stock), and simmer gently for a few more minutes until the lentils are a thick purée. Leave to cool.

3 Purée the mixture in a blender or food processor until smooth, then transfer to a bowl, cover and store in the refrigerator until needed.

Olive–Sun-dried Tomato–Lentil Spread

· · · · · · · · · · · · · ❤ · · · · · · · · · · · · ·

Makes 1 pint (600 ml)

An infusion of spring onions, sun-dried tomatoes, garlic, olives and chillies is one of my favourite flavour-bases. It adds a lively and delicate richness to split red lentils, just the thing for spreading on to crusty bread.

3 small spring onions, sliced

2 dry-packed sun-dried tomatoes, chopped (use scissors)

1 garlic clove, crushed

2–3 black olives in brine, drained and flesh slivered off the stones

pinch of crushed dried chillies

4 fl oz (100 ml) stock

8 oz (225 g) split red lentils, rinsed

1 pint (600 ml) salt-free stock or water

vegetable bouillon powder (optional)

1 Put the onions, tomatoes, garlic, olive slivers and chilli in a heavy-bottomed saucepan with the 4 fl oz (100 ml) stock. Bring to the boil, then reduce the heat and simmer briskly for a few minutes or until the onions are very tender and the liquid almost gone.

2 Stir in the red lentils and the salt-free stock or water. Simmer for 20–30 minutes or until the lentils are tender, adding more liquid if needed to prevent scorching. Season with salt and pepper (and add some vegetable bouillon powder if you have used water instead of salt-free stock) and simmer gently for a few more minutes until the lentils are a thick purée. Leave to cool.

3 Purée the mixture in a blender or food processor until smooth, then transfer to a bowl, cover and store in the refrigerator until needed.

Middle-Eastern Lentil Spread

· · · · · · · · · · · · · · · ·ⓥ· · · · · · · · · · · · · · ·

Makes   1   pint   (600   ml)

Lemon, cumin and coriander work well with red lentils. This version of lentil spread is particularly good as a dip with pita crisps (see page 46).

4 fl oz (100 ml) stock
juice of ¹/₂ lemon
³/₄ teaspoon ground cumin
³/₄ teaspoon ground coriander
pinch of cayenne pepper
3–4 spring onions, sliced
1–2 garlic cloves, crushed

8 oz (225 g) split red lentils, rinsed
about 1 pint (600 ml) salt-free stock or water
salt and freshly ground pepper
vegetable bouillon powder (optional)

1 Pour the 4 fl oz (100 ml) stock into a heavy-bottomed saucepan, and add the lemon juice, spices, onions and garlic. Bring to the boil, then reduce the heat and simmer for a few minutes until the onions are tender and the liquid almost gone.

2 Stir in the red lentils and the salt-free stock or water, and simmer for 20–30 minutes or until the lentils are tender. Add more liquid, if necessary, to prevent scorching. Season with salt and pepper (adding some vegetable bouillon powder if you have used water instead of salt-free stock), and simmer gently for a few more minutes until the lentils are a thick purée. Leave to cool.

3 Purée the mixture in a blender or food processor until smooth, then transfer to a bowl, cover and store in the refrigerator until required.

Spicy Bean Dip

· · · · · · · · · · · · · · **V** · **Z** · · · · · · · · · · · · · ·

Makes 1 ¹/₂ pints (900 ml)

A can of beans, a carton of passata (sieved tomatoes) and a bold hand with the seasonings give you a most delicious pot of beans. Purée them (as described in step 3) and eat, still warm, with vegetable dippers, or any of the crisps at the end of this chapter (see pages 46–8). Alternatively, purée only half of the mixture then mix with the unpuréed portion and wrap in wheat tortillas, garnished with Green Pea Dip (see page 37) and Creamy Herb Sauce (see page 192). Or dilute the half-puréed, half-unpuréed version with vegetable stock and serve as a soup. Or prepare only as far as step 2, and serve on toast. Or . . . but I'm sure you will come up with plenty of your own ideas. If you can't get hold of passata (though you'll find it in most supermarkets, either canned or in cartons), use a 14 oz (400 g) can of chopped tomatoes, puréed in the blender with 3 tablespoons tomato purée.

12 spring onions, sliced

3–4 garlic cloves, cut into chunks

3–4 dry-packed, sun-dried tomatoes, chopped (use scissors) (optional)

¹/₂ pint (300 ml) stock

3–4 fl oz (75–100 ml) dry white vermouth

1–2 generous pinches of ground cumin

1–2 generous pinches of crushed dried chillies

two 15 oz (432 g) cans of beans (borlotti, cannellini, pinto or red kidney), drained and rinsed

1 lb (500 g) carton of passata

salt and freshly ground pepper

2 tablespoons chopped fresh parsley

1–2 tablespoons chopped fresh coriander, shredded fresh mint or shredded fresh basil

juice of ¹/₂ lime

1 Put the onions, garlic, sun-dried tomatoes (if using), stock, vermouth, cumin and chilli in a heavy-bottomed saucepan. Cover, bring to the boil and boil for 5–7 minutes. Uncover and simmer briskly, stirring occasionally, until the liquid is reduced and syrupy, and the garlic meltingly tender.

2 Add the beans and stir to coat them with the onion–spice mixture. Stir in the passata and season with salt and pepper. Simmer, uncovered, for about 15 minutes or until thick. Stir in the chopped herbs and the lime juice. Leave to cool slightly.

3 Process the mixture to a rough purée in a blender or food processor, then transfer to a bowl and serve warm.

Cannellini–Red Pepper Dip

· · · · · · · · · · · · · · · · · ⓥ · · ⓩ · · · · · · · · · · · · · · · · ·

Makes 1 pint (600 ml)

More wonderful convenience food: canned cannellini (white kidney) beans and bottled or canned red peppers. They team up to make a beautifully blushing, compellingly creamy spread or dip. Dilute it with stock, add some chopped herbs, and it makes a quick and easy sauce for pasta or grains.

15 oz (432 g) can of cannellini beans

15 oz (432 g) can or jar of red peppers (pimentos)

1/4 teaspoon cumin seeds

3 garlic cloves, crushed

a good pinch of dried chilli flakes

4–5 dry-packed, sun-dried tomatoes, diced (with scissors) (optional)

1/2 pint (300 ml) stock

salt and freshly ground pepper

1 Empty the beans and the peppers into a colander. Rinse under cold running water and set aside to drain well.

2 Put the cumin seeds in a frying pan and heat gently for about 1 minute or until toasted and fragrant, stirring constantly. Add the garlic, chilli, tomatoes (if using) and stock. Cover, bring to the boil and boil for 3–4 minutes. Uncover and simmer until the garlic is tender and the liquid has reduced considerably and become syrupy.

3 Put the drained peppers and beans in a food processor, and scrape in the garlic–chilli infusion. Season with salt and pepper, then purée until smooth. Transfer to a bowl, cover and refrigerate until needed.

Hummus

· · · · · · · · · · · · · · · · **V** · · · · · · · · · · · · · · ·

Makes 1 pint (600 ml)

Hummus (chick pea spread) is usually made with tahini (sesame seed paste) and raw garlic, in addition to the basic chick pea purée. Sesame seeds are a high-fat food – in tahini they are concentrated. Some recipes for hummus call for olive oil as well, so, all in all, it can be a wickedly fattening dish. I use ½ tablespoon sesame seeds, and stock-sautéed garlic, in place of the more traditional raw garlic–tahini–olive oil mixture. The ½ tablespoon seeds adds just 2 grams of fat to the recipe (as opposed to the 28 grams of fat in 4 tablespoons tahini), and the stock-sautéed garlic adds a much gentler garlic flavour than raw garlic would. Add lemon juice to your taste – some like a very lemony Hummus, some don't.

½ tablespoon sesame seeds
juice of 1½–2 lemons
2 garlic cloves, crushed

¼ pint (150 ml) stock
two 15 oz (432 g) cans of chick peas

1 Put the sesame seeds in a heavy-bottomed frying pan, and heat gently for about 1 minute or until toasted and fragrant, stirring constantly.

2 Stir in the juice of ½ lemon, the garlic and stock, and bring to the boil. Cook, stirring, until the garlic is tender and the liquid almost gone.

3 Drain the chick peas, reserving their liquid. Put the sesame mixture in a blender or food processor, and add a quarter of the chick pea liquid. Process for a few moments, then add a quarter of the chick peas and process until smooth.

4 Add the juice of 1 lemon and the remaining chick peas. Process until the hummus has the delightful consistency of fluffy mashed potatoes. Taste, add more lemon juice if required, and process once more. Transfer to a bowl, cover and refrigerate until needed.

Yoghurt 'Cream' Cheese

Very low-fat yoghurt can be thin and watery. Remedy this by draining it overnight. The whey seeps away, leaving a thick, creamy, spreadable cheese. Instead of herbs, try crushed garlic marinated in a bit of white wine (or balsamic) vinegar. Or try a sweet spread – fold in a bit of honey or marmalade. This 'cheese' is delicious spread on bagels or toast and is excellent in sandwiches.

very low-fat natural yoghurt   chopped fresh herbs

1 Line a sieve with a double layer of muslin or a jelly bag. Place over a large bowl. Pour the yoghurt into the sieve, fold the cloth over the top and refrigerate overnight.

2 Next day, drain the liquid from the bowl, and rinse and dry the bowl. Scrape the drained yoghurt into the bowl and fold in the herbs. Cover and refrigerate until needed.

Beetroot–Chutney Dip

Makes ¹/₂ pint (300 ml)

If you crave edible fire, and you can find Tuscan Lemon Chutney or Lime–Chilli Chutney, try them in this recipe in place of mango chutney. Hot mango chutney is good, too, of course, but it will just tingle on the tongue, it won't try to blow the top of your head off. On the other hand, if your palate is not part-asbestos, use ordinary mango chutney in place of the hot version.

8 oz (225 g) natural cooked   2–3 tablespoons hot (spicy)
   beetroot (with no vinegar)   mango chutney

1 Cut the beetroot into chunks and put in a blender or food processor with the chutney. Process to a rough purée.

2 Transfer to a bowl, cover and store in the fridge until needed.

Dippers

The next three recipes make no-fat dippers for all your dips and spreads. Shop-bought crisps, tortilla chips, and so on, pile on the fat calories; making your own is easy and fun. Every oven is different, so take the timing given as a very general guide only, and the first time you make them, check them carefully – they might need more or less time.

Pita Crisps

· · · · · · · · · · · · · · ⓥ · · · · · · · · · · · · · ·

brown or white pita breads

1 Preheat the oven to 300°F, 150°C, Gas Mark 2.

2 With kitchen scissors, cut the pita breads into quarters or eighths, then separate each piece into two. Arrange in one layer on a non-stick baking sheet, and bake in the oven for 10–15 minutes or until dried out and crisp. They will keep for several weeks in an airtight container.

Tortilla Chips

* * * * * * * * * * * * * *  * * * * * * * * * * * *

Maize tortillas are wonderfully versatile and a delicious Mexican food. They resemble chapattis made from maize meal, and contain no fat whatsoever. Many supermarkets now stock maize tortillas; you should find them on the shelves with the packaged bread or with ethnic foods.

corn (maize) tortillas

1 Preheat the oven to 300°F, 150°C, Gas Mark 2.

2 Bake the tortillas directly on the oven shelf for 15–20 minutes, turning once, until crisp right through (they will break with a clean 'snap'). Break into quarters or eighths, cool and store in an airtight container (they will keep for a month or more).

MICROWAVE METHOD

1 Put a double layer of absorbent kitchen paper on the microwave turntable.

2 Arrange five tortillas on the paper around the outside of the turntable. They should not quite touch each other. Microwave on high (100%) for 2–2^1/$_2$ minutes.

3 If the towels are wet, replace them. Turn the tortillas over and microwave on high (100%) for another 2–2^1/$_2$ minutes.

4 Place the tortillas on a wire rack and leave to rest for 5 minutes. Break into quarters or eighths, cool and store in an airtight container.

Potato Crisps

· · · · · · · · · · · V · · · · · · · · · · ·

Makes about 50 crisps

Home-made potato crisps? Why not? Think of the luxury – pure potato, minimal grease. What bliss! For even easier crisps (if you have a microwave), try to find the clever crisp-maker (it looks like a circular mini-toast-rack) designed specifically for the microwave. All you do is slice the potatoes paper-thin, slot the slices into the rack and microwave for a few minutes. The resulting crisps are totally fat-free and amazingly good. Look for the gadget (it costs less than £5) in cookware shops, department stores and mail-order catalogues (such as Lakeland Plastics).

1 large baking potato (King Edward or Maris Piper), about 10 oz (275 g)

oil and water spray (see page 5)
salt (optional)

1 Preheat the oven to 350°F, 180°C, Gas Mark 4.

2 Slice the potato paper-thin, using a mandoline, if you have one, or the slicing disk of a food processor, or the slicing slot on an old-fashioned grater.

3 Arrange the slices in a single layer on two non-stick baking sheets that you have misted lightly with oil spray. Salt lightly, if desired. Bake in the oven for about 15 minutes. Re-position the crisps on the sheets, and reposition the sheets in the oven, if necessary, to ensure even browning, and bake for another 3–5 minutes or until the potato slices are crisp and browned, but not burnt.

Poached Mushrooms
for Stuffing or Dipping

· · · · · · · · · · · · · · ·Ⓥ· ·Ⓩ· · · · · · · · · · · · · ·

*A platter of chicory leaves, red, yellow and green peppers (trimmed
and cut into little boats), and these mushroom caps, all filled with a
colourful variety of dips and spreads, makes an arresting edible
display for a buffet table. As a design statement they only have a
moment of glory; when the hungry hordes attack, the platter empties
very quickly. If you don't feel like stuffing all those little morsels, put
a selection of colourful dips and spreads into pretty bowls. Place on a
large platter, and surround with heaps of chicory leaves, pepper boats
and mushroom caps.*

about 12 oz–1 lb (350–450 g)
 firm, white, medium-sized or
 button mushrooms
about 3 fl oz (75 ml) stock

about 3 fl oz (75 ml) dry sherry
1–2 dashes of Teriyaki sauce

1 Carefully remove the stems from the mushroom caps. Save the stems
for another use (Duxelles or Mushroom Ragout, see pages 36 and 167,
for instance). With a teaspoon, gently even out the mushroom cap
opening so it will hold a filling nicely.

2 Pour the stock, sherry and Teriyaki sauce into a non-stick frying pan
that will hold the mushroom caps in one layer. Bring the liquid to the
boil, add the mushroom caps in one layer, open-sides up, reduce the
heat, cover and simmer for 2–3 minutes. Uncover, raise the heat and
cook, tossing the mushrooms in the pan, for a minute or so or until the
caps are cooked but still quite firm, and the liquid is reduced and
syrupy. Remove the mushroom caps from the pan, and drain upside-
down on absorbent kitchen paper. Allow to cool before stuffing.

Grains

Complex carbohydrate, fibre, protein, essential fatty acids, fat-soluble vitamins – grains have them all. Combined with beans, grains form a high-quality protein, which is why old favourites from around the world, like baked beans on toast, tortillas and beans, minestrone soup (with macaroni and beans), red beans and rice, Moors and Christians (black beans and rice), and so on, nourish entire populations. Although these classics combine beans and grains in the same meal, it is not necessary always to eat them together. If you eat both beans and grains frequently, their protein will complement each other even if they are consumed at different times.

The most familiar grains are rice and wheat (in the form of pasta, bread and breakfast cereals), but there is a world of additional choices. Check out the supermarket and the wholefood shop, and cast your eyes over the bounty: buckwheat, millet, couscous, cracked wheat, wild rice (the most luxurious grain of all). What feasting lies in store! Keep this in mind: the less processing, the more nutrition, so, whenever possible, choose the whole grain.

I find the easiest way to measure grains, cooked or raw, is with a measuring jug: ¹/₄–¹/₂ pint (150–300 ml) cooked grain constitutes a side dish serving; 1–1¹/₄ pints (600–750 ml), a main dish serving. As always, be flexible: one person's satisfying meal is another's tantalising taste, and yet another's painful over-indulgence!

As far as pasta is concerned, conventional wisdom advises 2 oz (50 g) (raw weight) pasta per serving, but I find this totally absurd. For a main course, 4–8 oz (100–225 g) is more like it, but, as always, use your appetite as a guide.

Rice

Brown rice bursts with nutrients and has a superb taste and texture: nutty, chewy, not to mention deeply comforting and satisfying. I think cooked brown rice makes a wonderful breakfast: mix in a handful of sultanas or chopped dried fruit (try dried mango – what a treat!) and pour some warm skimmed milk over it into which you have mixed some skimmed milk powder for extra richness and nutrition.

To cook brown rice (both short- and long-grain)

Rice will expand to three times its volume when cooked. Measure the uncooked rice by pouring it into a measuring jug: ¹/₂ pint (300 ml) rice will yield 1¹/₂ pints (900 ml) cooked rice. Choose a heavy-bottomed saucepan (with room for the rice to expand) that can be covered tightly. Measure the rice first, then rinse it in a sieve under cold running water. Pour the rice into the pan, then pour in twice the volume of stock or water. In other words, for ¹/₂ pint (300 ml) raw rice, add 1 pint (600 ml) liquid. Add some salt and a bay leaf, and bring to the boil. Stir once, cover tightly, reduce the heat, and simmer over very low heat for 45–55 minutes for long grain, 35–40 minutes for short-grain. (The exact timing depends on the rice, your cooker, and the thickness of the pan.) Uncover, fluff with a fork, drape with a clean tea-towel, re-cover over the tea-towel, and leave, off the heat, for 10 minutes. By now the rice will be tender and fluffy, and the liquid absorbed.

Pan-Fried Wild Rice Fritters

Makes 6

Leftover wild rice is gastronomic treasure. It always pays to make too much (although you may have to hide it to ensure that there are leftovers). I love these hot fritters for breakfast, or serve them in an overlapping circle surrounding a vegetable stew or a heap of spicy beans.

½ pint (300 ml) cooked wild rice
 (see page 54)
2 egg whites, lightly beaten

olive oil and water spray (see
 page 5)

1 Stir the wild rice into the lightly beaten egg white.

2 Mist a non-stick frying pan with the oil spray and heat. Drop the wild rice mixture, in rounded tablespoonfuls, into the pan, and flatten with a broad spatula. Pan-fry until set on one side, then slide the spatula beneath each fritter to loosen, and carefully turn them over. Cook on the second side until both sides are crisp and golden. Transfer to a warm plate, tent loosely with foil to keep warm. Repeat until the rice mixture is used, making about six fritters.

Pan-Fried Brown Rice Fritters

· ·

Makes 6

Good enough reason to keep cooked rice on hand, these adorable little fritters are pan-fried in a non-stick frying pan with a bare misting of oil.

³/₄ pint (450 ml) cooked short-
   grain brown rice (see page 51)
2 egg whites, lightly beaten
salt and freshly ground pepper

1–1¹/₂ tablespoons grated
   Parmesan cheese
olive oil and water spray (see
   page 5)

1 Stir the rice into the lightly beaten egg white and season with salt and pepper. Toss with two spoons to combine thoroughly, and to break up any clumps of rice. Stir in the cheese.

2 Mist a non-stick frying pan with the oil spray and heat. Drop the rice mixture, in rounded tablespoonfuls, into the pan, and flatten with a broad spatula. Pan-fry until completely set on one side, then carefully slide the spatula under to loosen and flip over the fritters. Pan-fry until cooked through and golden on both sides. Transfer to a warm plate and tent loosely with foil to keep warm while making remaining fritters. Repeat until the rice batter is used, making about six fritters.

Wild Rice Pilaff

. . . .

Makes 1 1/2 pints (900 ml)

Wild rice is not a rice at all, but a native American aquatic wild grass, Zizania aquatica. Although wild rice is now cultivated in California, at one time the truly wild variety was the only one available. The really wild stuff grows in abundance in parts of Minnesota and Wisconsin, and is gathered there with laborious care by native Americans. They canoe down the narrow watery paths that meander through the tall grain, flailing away at the stalks, until the canoe is full of the precious seeds. Centuries ago, the Ojibway Indians called it mahnomen (good grain) and the early French explorers of the New World called it folle avoine *(crazy oat).*

Cook wild rice grains until they begin to puff open. Some of the grains will remain closed; it is the contrast between the two that gives a dish of wild rice such wonderful texture. Be sure not to overcook it, however – some of the grains should remain al dente *to be interesting. During the cooking, be prepared to be flexible; some batches cook quicker than others. Wild rice is available from good wholefood shops, speciality stores and some supermarkets.*

1½ pints (900 ml) stock
2 carrots, finely chopped
5 spring onions, thinly sliced
½ pint (300 ml), about 8 oz
  (225 g) raw wild rice

¼ teaspoon chopped fresh
  thyme or a pinch of dried
  thyme
I bay leaf
salt and freshly ground pepper

I Preheat the oven to 350°F, 180°C, Gas Mark 4.

2 Put ½ pint (300 ml) of the stock in a flameproof casserole that can be covered. Add the carrots and spring onions and bring to the boil. Reduce the heat, cover and simmer until the vegetables are tender and the liquid almost gone. Add the wild rice and stir so that the vegetables and rice are well combined. Add the remaining stock and the herbs, and season with salt and pepper. Bring back to the boil, then cover and

bake in the oven for 45–55 minutes or until all the liquid is absorbed, and the wild rice cooked (it should remain somewhat crunchy). Remove from the oven, lift off the lid and drape a clean tea-towel over the open pan. Replace the lid over the towel and leave for 5–10 minutes. Remove the bay leaf before serving.

Rice with Spring Onions and Vermouth

. . . .

Makes 1 pint (600 ml)

This is a kind of instant risotto – it's ridiculously easy to make (if you have the cooked rice on hand) and, as with most rice dishes, it is extremely comforting. Make it into a complete meal by stirring in some stir-fried or steamed asparagus tips, some lightly cooked fresh or frozen peas and some chopped fresh herbs.

4 fl oz (100 ml) dry white vermouth
4 fl oz (100 ml) stock
6 spring onions, sliced
1 pint (600 ml) cooked short-grain brown rice (see page 51)

salt and freshly ground pepper
2–3 tablespoons grated Parmesan cheese (optional)

1 Put the vermouth, stock and spring onions in a frying pan. Bring to the boil, then reduce the heat and simmer until the liquid is reduced by half.

2 Stir in the rice, season with salt and pepper, and cook, stirring, over gentle heat until the rice is soft and thoroughly hot. Serve at once or, if you wish, sprinkle in the cheese, stir and cook over the lowest heat until the cheese has melted into the rice.

V Omit the Parmesan

Spinach–Rice Pie

Serves 4 – 6

Add mozzarella cheese to a rice crust mixture, and fill the baked crust with vividly flavoured spinach for a glorious main dish. The recipe below makes more spinach than you need to fill the crust. It's so good, you may find that you've polished it off all by yourself as you prepare the meal; if not, use it to fill filo rolls or triangles (see page 195), serve it as a side vegetable at another meal, or cook it in a frittata (see page 178).

BASE

1 pint (600 ml) well-seasoned cooked short-grain brown rice (see page 51)

2 egg whites, lightly beaten

4–5 oz (100–150 g) half-fat mozzarella cheese, drained and shredded

olive oil and water spray (see page 5)

FILLING

1 bag (about 2 lb/900 g) frozen chopped spinach, thawed

6 spring onions, sliced

2–3 dry-packed sun-dried tomatoes, chopped (use scissors)

3 black olives in brine, drained and flesh slivered off the stones

1–2 garlic cloves, crushed

1/2 pint (300 ml) stock

salt and freshly ground pepper

1 tablespoon tomato purée

5 tablespoons grated Parmesan cheese

1 Preheat the oven to 425°F, 220°C, Gas Mark 7.

2 Put the rice, egg white and mozzarella cheese in a bowl. Toss with two spoons to mix thoroughly and to break up any clumps of rice. Mist an 11 inch (28 cm) non-stick flan dish with the oil spray, and tip the rice into the dish. Use the back of a large spoon to spread it evenly over the bottom and up the sides of the dish. Bake for 20 minutes.

3 Meanwhile, drain the spinach in a colander and squeeze it as dry as possible. Set aside.

4 Put the spring onions, sun-dried tomatoes, olives, garlic and stock in a frying pan. Bring to the boil, then reduce the heat and simmer until the onions are tender and the liquid almost gone. Stir in the spinach and season well with salt and pepper. Stir and cook for a few minutes or until the spinach is hot and cooked. (It won't take long so take care not to overcook.) Stir in the tomato purée and 2 tablespoons of the Parmesan cheese.

5 Spread the spinach mixture in the cooked rice crust. (You will have more than you need; save the rest for another meal.) Sprinkle evenly with the remaining Parmesan cheese, then flash under a hot grill for 2–3 minutes or until the cheese is melted and bubbly.

VARIATION
Rice 'Pizza'

Spread the rice crust with warm tomato sauce (see page 91), sprinkle with shredded half-fat mozzarella, and flash under the grill until the cheese melts. The crust under the sauce softens up, but the surrounding edges become crunchy and the molten cheese adds a creamy dimension. It is a most seductive combination.

Mushroom Pie

. . . .

Serves 6

A mixture of cooked brown rice and lightly beaten egg white can be used to line a flan dish and baked to form a nutritious and delicious pie crust. The rice crust can be filled with almost any savoury mixture: here I've used a creamy mushroom ragout.

2 egg whites
½ tablespoon Dijon mustard
2 pints (1.1 litres) well-seasoned cooked brown rice (see page 51)

oil and water spray (see page 5)
Creamy Mushroom Ragout (see page 167), warmed

1 Preheat the oven to 425°F, 220°C, Gas Mark 7.

2 Lightly beat the egg whites with the mustard. Stir in the rice, and toss with two spoons to combine well and to break up any clumps of rice. Mist a non-stick 11 inch (28 cm) flan dish with the oil spray, and scrape the rice mixture into the dish. With the back of a large spoon, press the rice over the bottom and up the sides of the dish. Bake in the oven for 20 minutes.

3 Spoon the Mushroom Ragout into the rice crust and serve at once.

Top to bottom Colourful Corn Chowder (page 25), Chunky Grilled Pepper Gazpacho with Tomato Sorbet (page 31) and Olive-Sun-dried Tomato-Lentil Spread (page 40)

Opposite page 59, clockwise from top Stir-Fried Asparagus (page 154), Pan-Fried Wild Rice Fritters (page 52) and Pan-Fried Brown Rice Fritters (page 53) on a plate with Creamy Mushroom Ragout (page 167) and Cherry Tomato and Cucumber Relish (page 188)

Rice and Grilled Vegetable Pie

· ·

Serves 4 – 6

Based on a traditional Italian recipe, this pie is much leaner than the original, although it retains the characteristic flavour and appearance. A wedge of this and a salad make an incomparable evening meal. It's good warm or at room temperature (or straight out of the fridge – I know!).

olive oil and water spray (see page 5)

4 tablespoons breadcrumbs

5 tablespoons grated Parmesan cheese

2 pints (1.1 litres) cooked brown rice (see page 51)

1 pint (600 ml) tomato sauce (see pages 91 and 92)

2 aubergines, sliced and grilled (see page 129)

5 courgettes, sliced and grilled (see page 130)

1 Preheat the oven to 425°F, 220°C, Gas Mark 7.

2 Mist an 11 inch (28 cm) non-stick flan tin with oil spray. Mix the breadcrumbs with 2 tablespoons of the Parmesan cheese. Spoon this mixture into the tin, and shake the tin to spread the crumbs all over the bottom. Tilt the tin so the crumbs coat the sides.

3 Mix the rice with the tomato sauce and the remaining cheese. Spread half this mixture over the bottom and up the sides of the flan tin. Arrange the grilled vegetables, in one overlapping layer of slices, on the rice base, then spread the remaining rice mixture over the vegetables. Sprinkle evenly with the remaining breadcrumb mixture. Mist the top very lightly with the olive oil spray.

4 Bake in the oven for 20–30 minutes or until the top is golden brown, and the pie is slightly puffy and bubbly. Remove from the oven and leave on a rack for 5–10 minutes before cutting into wedges.

Sweet Rice Pulao

. . . . V . . . .

Makes 1 ¹/₂ pints (900 ml)

This is the perfect partner for the vegetable curries on pages 156–62, along with Raita (see pages 191–2) and Green Split Pea Dhal (see page 113). Arrange it all on a large white platter to show it off: colour, texture, flavour, temperature contrast – all the things I love in a meal – leap off the platter.

1 ¹/₂ pints (900 ml) stock
juice of ¹/₂ lemon and ¹/₂ orange
¹/₂ inch (1 cm) piece of fresh root ginger, peeled and crushed
1 red or yellow pepper, peeled, deseeded and chopped
2 small onions, chopped
2 carrots, chopped
¹/₄ teaspoon each of ground cinnamon, ground coriander and ground turmeric

1 small bay leaf
¹/₈ teaspoon ground allspice
two 14 oz (400 g) cans of tomatoes, well drained, deseeded and chopped
2 tablespoons raisins
2 tablespoons chopped no-soak dried apricots
¹/₂ pint (300 ml) raw long-grain brown rice
salt and freshly ground pepper

1 Put ¹/₂ pint (300 ml) of the stock, the fruit juices, ginger, vegetables and spices in a flameproof casserole or heavy-bottomed saucepan. Bring to the boil, cover, reduce the heat and simmer for 5 minutes. Uncover and simmer for 3–5 minutes more or until the vegetables are tender, and the liquid almost gone. Stir in the tomatoes and dried fruits, and simmer, stirring, for a few minutes or until the mixture has thickened.

2 Add the rice and stir to combine well. Stir in the remaining stock, season liberally with salt and pepper, and bring to the boil. Reduce the heat, cover the pan and leave to simmer very gently for 40–45 minutes. Remove from the heat. Uncover and fluff up the rice with a fork. Drape a clean tea-towel over the open pan, replace the lid over the tea-towel, and leave to stand for 5–10 minutes. Remove and discard the bay leaf before serving.

Moulded Rice Pulao with Stir-Fried Peppers

Serves 6

Mould the colourful rice in a teacup, then unmould it on to a pretty plate. Surround with stir-fried peppers for a knock-out dinner party accompaniment.

warm Sweet Rice Pulao (see page 60)
2 red peppers
2 yellow peppers
½ pint (300 ml) stock
good pinch of ground cumin

good pinch of ground coriander
salt and freshly ground pepper
lemon or lime and orange wedges, chopped fresh parsley and chopped fresh coriander, to serve

1 Pack the warm rice pulao into teacups, cover with cling film and set aside.

2 Halve the peppers and remove their stems, seeds and ribs. Cut the peppers lengthways into their natural sections, and peel them with a swivel-bladed vegetable peeler. Cut the sections into ½ inch (1 cm) wide strips.

3 Put the pepper strips in a frying pan, add the stock, and season with the spices, salt and pepper. Bring to the boil, then reduce the heat and simmer briskly, stirring frequently, until the peppers are tender and bathed in a syrupy glaze.

4 To serve, unmould the rice on to individual plates. (To do this, remove the cling film, put a plate over a teacup, turn over, give it a good shake and the moulded rice will slide out.) Surround each mound of rice with a wreath of warm or cold peppers, add 2–3 small wedges of lemon or lime and orange, and sprinkle over chopped herbs.

Brown Rice Salad with Cauliflower

. . . .

Makes 2¹/₂ pints (1.4 litres)

The ivory of the cauliflower and the dressing, and the brown of the rice make for a rather muted appearance, but the garnish of Cherry Tomato and Cucumber Relish and chopped herbs adds a jolt of colour. If you wish, use halved cherry tomatoes in place of the relish.

2 fl oz (50 ml) balsamic vinegar

juice of I large lemon

I teaspoon sugar

2–3 dashes of Teriyaki sauce

I pint (600 ml) warm, cooked long-grain brown rice (see page 51)

I small cauliflower, about I lb (450 g), separated into florets and steamed

salt and freshly ground pepper

3 tablespoons no-fat fromage frais

2 tablespoons 97 per cent fat-free mayonnaise-style dressing

1¹/₂ teaspoons Dijon mustard

1–2 tablespoons snipped fresh chives

1–2 tablespoons chopped fresh parsley

Cherry Tomato and Cucumber Relish (see page 188), to serve

1 Mix the vinegar, lemon juice, sugar and Teriyaki sauce, and add to the rice. Toss with two spoons to coat the rice thoroughly, and to break up any clumps of rice. Toss in the cauliflower, and season with salt and pepper.

2 Whisk together the fromage frais, mayonnaise and Dijon mustard. Fold this mixture into the rice and cauliflower, then fold in the herbs. To serve, arrange on a platter, and surround with Cherry Tomato and Cucumber Relish.

Smoked Tofu Kedgeree

· · · · · · · · · · · · · ◊ · · · · · · · · · · · · ·

Makes 2 pints (1.1 litres)

Here, stock stands in for butter, and smoked tofu for haddock, to make a stunning dish. The gentle smokiness of the tofu and spiciness of the garam masala work well together. Tofu is made from soya beans. Of all the available beans, soya beans have the most (and the highest-quality) protein. They also have the highest fat content, but are still a comparatively low-fat food. Tofu is, essentially, soya bean cheese; it is made from curdled soya milk in much the same way as dairy cheese is made from dairy milk. The blandness of tofu, and its slightly spongy texture, means that it soaks up the flavours of infusions and dressings extremely well.

8 fl oz (225 ml) stock

3 red peppers, peeled, deseeded and chopped

2 tablespoons skimmed milk powder

4 fl oz (100 ml) skimmed milk

1 tablespoon garam masala

1/2 pint (300 ml) frozen sweetcorn

1/2 pint (300 ml) frozen peas

1/2 pint (300 ml) cooked long-grain brown rice (see page 51)

8 oz (220 g) package of smoked tofu, cut into 1 inch (2.5 cm) cubes

salt and freshly ground pepper

chopped fresh parsley, to serve

1 Put the stock and peppers in a large, heavy-bottomed frying pan. Bring to the boil, then reduce the heat and simmer until the peppers are tender and the liquid greatly reduced and syrupy. Mix the skimmed milk powder into the milk, and stir into the peppers with the garam masala. Simmer very gently for 1–2 minutes, stirring.

2 Add the vegetables to the pan, and cook, for a few minutes, stirring, until the vegetables are warmed through and cooked. Add the rice, and stir until everything is well combined.

3 Add the tofu, and season with salt and pepper. Cook, stirring gently for a few moments (be careful not to break up the tofu) until heated through. Serve, sprinkled with parsley.

Brown Rice Salad
with Broccoli

. . . . Ⓥ . . . .

Makes 2 ¹/₂ pints (1.4 litres)

Here, rice and broccoli are dressed with an Oriental-style mixture of citrus juice, Teriyaki and sugar, with a little balsamic vinegar to jazz it up. If you dress the rice while it is still warm, the flavours soak in most efficiently.

1 lb (450 g) broccoli
2 pints (1.1 litres) warm, cooked
   long-grain brown rice (see page
   51)
cherry tomatoes, halved and
   fresh coriander leaves, to serve

DRESSING
juice of 3 large oranges

juice of 3 limes
3 tablespoons Teriyaki sauce
2 tablespoons balsamic vinegar
3 teaspoons sugar
¹/₂ inch (1 cm) piece of fresh root
   ginger, peeled and crushed
1 garlic clove, crushed

1 Whisk all the dressing ingredients together in a small jug, and set aside.

2 Cut the florets from the broccoli and put them in a steamer basket. Trim away and discard the tough woody bottoms of the stalks, peel the stalks, and quarter them lengthways. Add the stalks to the steamer basket. Steam over boiling water for about 10 minutes or until 'crisp–tender' – in other words, it should still have a bit of a crunch and remain bright green. Rinse under cold running water to set the colour, drain well, and set aside to cool.

3 Put the rice in a large bowl and pour over half the dressing. Toss with two spoons to mix well, and to break up any clumps of rice. Toss the cooled broccoli with the remaining dressing, then gently fold the broccoli into the rice. Serve spread out on a platter, surrounded by halved cherry tomatoes and sprinkled with coriander leaves.

Bulghur

Tabouli

· · · · · · · · · · · · · ○ · · · · · · · · · · · · ·

Makes 2¹/₂ pints (1.4 litres)

Tabouli is a refreshing and colourful salad of herbs, tomatoes and grain (bulghur wheat). The success of the dish depends on the tomatoes; they must be ripe and bursting with flavour. Some marketing genius has tumbled to the fact that flavourful food is a good money-spinner, so it is often possible these days to buy a supermarket tomato – even out of season – that actually tastes like a tomato. They are sometimes labelled 'grown for flavour'. It's best to buy tomatoes a few days (even a week) ahead of time, and then to let them sit in the kitchen for the flavour to develop. If you can't find large, tasty tomatoes, this salad will also work with halved cherry tomatoes.

8 oz (225 g) bulghur wheat
4 fl oz (100 ml) lemon juice
2 bunches of fresh parsley, finely chopped
8 spring onions, finely chopped

1 bunch of fresh mint, finely chopped
2 lb (900 g) ripe tomatoes, peeled, deseeded and chopped
salt and freshly ground pepper

1 Put the bulghur wheat in a large bowl, cover with boiling water and leave to soak for 30 minutes. Squeeze the grain with your hands to drain it, and place it in a clean bowl.

2 Stir in all the remaining ingredients, and mix well. Leave to stand for at least 1 hour before serving.

Bulghur Pilaff with Vegetables

· · · · · · · · · · · · · · ⓥ · · · · · · · · · · · · · ·

Makes 1 ¹/₂ pints (900 ml)

Bulghur is cracked wheat that can be 'cooked' by soaking in liquid (see Tabouli, page 65), or by the absorption method, like rice. It can be served as a main dish, but it also goes well with anything that rice goes with. If you eat a lot of rice, bulghur makes a nice occasional change.

I large mild onion, coarsely chopped

2–3 garlic cloves, crushed

I carrot, coarsely chopped

I pint (600 ml) stock

I red pepper, peeled, deseeded and chopped

I small courgette, coarsely chopped

I bunch of fresh chives, snipped

3 tablespoons chopped fresh parsley

2 tablespoons shredded fresh mint

salt and freshly ground pepper

7 oz (200 g) bulghur wheat

1 Put the onion, garlic, carrot and ¹/₂ pint (300 ml) of the stock in a heavy frying pan that can be covered. Cover, bring to the boil, and boil for 5–7 minutes. Uncover, reduce the heat slightly, and simmer briskly until the onion is tender and the liquid almost gone. Add the red pepper and courgette, and a splash more stock, and cook for a few minutes more.

2 Bring the remaining stock to the boil. Stir the herbs into the vegetables and season with salt and pepper. Add the bulghur, and stir so everything is well combined. Pour in the boiling stock, and stir well.

3 Cover the pan and simmer over the lowest possible heat for about 20 minutes or until the bulghur is tender but not mushy, and all the liquid is absorbed. Fluff with a fork, taste and adjust the seasonings, then remove from the heat. Remove the lid, drape a tea-towel over the open pan, and replace the lid on the pan, over the tea-towel. Leave to stand for 10–15 minutes.

Orange-Scented Bulghur

· · · · · · · · · · · · · **V** · · · · · · · · · · · ·

Makes 1 ¹/₂ pints (900 ml)

This is my favourite cracked wheat recipe. My assistant and I once cooked it for 250 people – when the banquet was over there wasn't a single grain left.

1 mild onion, coarsely chopped
¹/₂ pint (300 ml) stock
¹/₂ teaspoon ground coriander
¹/₂ teaspoon ground cumin
2 garlic cloves, chopped
¹/₂ large orange

6 oz (175 g) bulghur wheat
¹/₂ pint (300 ml) orange juice, strained
salt and freshly ground pepper
1–2 tablespoons chopped fresh coriander (optional)

1 Put the onion, 4 fl oz (100 ml) of the stock, the spices and garlic in a frying pan that can be covered. Bring to the boil, then reduce the heat and simmer until the liquid has greatly reduced and the onions are 'frying' in their own juices. Grate the zest from the orange right over the onions, so that some of the orange oils are added with the zest. Add the bulghur, and stir until everything is well combined. Bring the remaining stock to the boil with the orange juice, and stir it into the wheat. Season with salt and pepper.

2 Cover the pan and simmer over the lowest heat for about 20 minutes or until the bulghur is tender but not mushy, and all the liquid is absorbed. Fluff with a fork and remove from the heat. Drape a clean tea-towel over the open pan, and replace the lid over the towel. Leave to stand for 5–10 minutes. Sprinkle over the coriander before serving.

Spicy Bulghur, Bean and Vegetable Casserole

Makes 3 1/2 pints (2 litres)

For hearty appetites, this is a chilli-like vegetable stew cooked with a generous measure of cracked wheat. Serve in capacious soup bowls, and let everyone top their portion with their own selection of garnishes.

5 oz (150 g) bulghur wheat

1 pint (600 ml) boiling stock

1 large mild onion, coarsely chopped

3 celery stalks, cut into 1/2 inch (1 cm) slices

3 carrots, coarsely chopped

3 peppers, peeled, deseeded and coarsely chopped (1 red, 1 yellow and 1 green if available)

4 garlic cloves, crushed

1 tablespoon mild chilli powder (or to taste)

1/2 teaspoon ground coriander

2 teaspoons ground cumin

1/2 teaspoon paprika

two 14 oz (400 g) cans of chopped tomatoes

15 oz (432 g) can of red kidney beans, drained and rinsed

15 oz (432 g) can of chick peas, drained and rinsed

1 large cauliflower, separated into florets

salt and freshly ground pepper

TO GARNISH

fromage frais

grated Parmesan cheese

chopped fresh coriander

1 Combine the bulghur with 8 fl oz (225 ml) of the hot stock in a bowl, cover and set aside.

2 Put the vegetables, 1/2 pint (300 ml) of the remaining stock, and the spices in a flameproof casserole. Bring to the boil, then reduce the heat and simmer briskly, stirring, until the vegetables and spices are 'frying' in their own juices, and the vegetables are tender.

3 Stir in the tomatoes, bulghur, kidney beans, chick peas and cauliflower, and season with salt and pepper. Simmer, partially covered, for 30 minutes or until the mixture is thick and the cauliflower tender but not mushy. Arrange garnishes in bowls and serve with the casserole.

(V) Omit the fromage frais garnish

Couscous

Couscous is made up of tiny bits of semolina: you might say that it is a collection of tiny grains of pasta. Because most packaged couscous that you find in supermarkets and wholefood shops is precooked, it needs only a brief soaking in hot liquid. Couscous is an excellent accompaniment to any vegetable stew.

Basic Couscous

· · · · · · · · · · · · · ◊ · · · · · · · · · · · · ·

Makes 2 pints (1.1 litres)

12 oz (350 g) couscous
16 fl oz (475 ml) well-seasoned
  boiling stock

1 Combine the couscous and boiling liquid in a large bowl, and leave to soak for 10–15 minutes or until the liquid is absorbed and the grains tender. Fluff with a fork.

Couscous with Vegetable Curry

Makes 3 pints (1.75 litres)

1¼ pints (750 ml) stock

1 large mild onion, coarsely chopped

2–3 garlic cloves, crushed

1½ teaspoons ground cumin

1½ teaspoons ground coriander

¼ teaspoon ground allspice

¼ teaspoon cayenne pepper

½ teaspoon ground ginger

1 teaspoon ground tumeric

1 teaspoon paprika

3 celery stalks, cut into ½ inch (1 cm) slices

3 carrots, coarsely chopped

3 small white turnips, coarsely chopped

3 peppers (1 red, 1 green, 1 yellow) peeled, deseeded and coarsely chopped

1 fennel bulb, cut into ½ inch (1 cm) slices

15 oz (432 g) can of chick peas, drained and rinsed

6 tablespoons lemon juice

salt and freshly ground pepper

one quantity Basic Couscous (see page 69)

4 tablespoons chopped fresh parsley

2 tablespoons chopped fresh coriander

1 Put ½ pint (300 ml) of the stock, the onions, garlic and spices in a frying pan. Cover, bring to the boil, and boil for 5 minutes. Stir in the celery, carrots, turnips, peppers, fennel and another 2 fl oz (50 ml) of the stock. Simmer, stirring frequently, until the vegetables and spices are 'frying' in their own juices.

2 Stir in the remaining ingredients (except the herbs and couscous), including the remaining 13 fl oz (375 ml) stock. Season to taste with salt and pepper, then cover and simmer gently for 15 minutes.

3 Arrange the cooked couscous in a mound on a large platter, and surround with the vegetables. Sprinkle with the herbs.

Couscous Salad

Makes 2 ¹/₂ pints (1.4 litres)

This is one of my standbys for low-fat luncheon buffets. It is very easy to make, looks beautiful on the table, and seems to please most people – even those who have never had couscous before.

8 fl oz (225 ml) boiling, well-seasoned stock

6 oz (175 g) couscous

15 oz (432 g) can of chick peas, drained and rinsed

1 red pepper, peeled, deseeded and diced

3–4 spring onions, sliced thinly

1 small courgette, diced

1 small carrot, diced

3–4 tablespoons chopped fresh parsley

3–4 tablespoons shredded fresh mint

freshly ground pepper

DRESSING

¹/₂ pint (300 ml) stock

1¹/₂ –2¹/₂ tablespoons balsamic vinegar

1–2 limes

2 garlic cloves, crushed

¹/₂ teaspoon ground cumin

1–2 pinches of cayenne pepper

1 To make the dressing, put half the stock in a small frying pan, and add ¹/₂ tablespoon balsamic vinegar, the juice of ¹/₂ lime, the garlic, cumin and cayenne. Cover, bring to the boil, and boil for 5 minutes. Uncover, reduce the heat slightly, and simmer briskly until the garlic is very tender, and the liquid has cooked down to a syrupy glaze.

2 Add the remaining stock and boil until reduced by about half. Stir in a further 1 tablespoon balsamic vinegar and the juice of ¹/₂ lime. Keep warm.

3 For the salad, mix the boiling stock and couscous together in a large bowl. Cover with cling film and leave to stand for 10 minutes. Uncover, and fluff up with a fork.

4 Toss in all the remaining ingredients, except the dressing, and season with pepper.

5 Pour the warm dressing over the couscous and toss with two spoons. Taste and add more seasonings, vinegar and lime juice, if necessary.

Couscous Salad with Smoked Tofu and Oranges

· · · · · · · · · · · · · · · **V** · · · · · · · · · · · · · ·

Makes 2 pints (1.1 litres)

Oranges, smoked tofu, and fresh and spicy citrus dressing enhance the tender, wheaty couscous grains.

COUSCOUS

juice and finely grated zest of half a lime and half an orange

about 6 fl oz (175 ml) well-seasoned stock

6 oz (175 g) couscous

salt and freshly ground pepper

DRESSING

2 tablespoons balsamic vinegar

2 tablespoons lime juice

2 tablespoons orange juice

1 teaspoon soy sauce

several dashes of Tabasco sauce

several dashes of Teriyaki sauce

1 garlic clove, crushed (optional)

SALAD

1 large seedless orange, peeled of all skin and pith, and diced

8 oz (220 g) smoked Tofu, cut into 1/2 inch (1 cm) cubes

2 tablespoons chopped fresh parsley

4 spring onions, sliced

2 tablespoons shredded fresh mint

GARNISH

halved cherry tomatoes

small wedges of lemon, lime and orange

1 For the couscous, mix the lime juice, orange juice and grated zests in a measuring jug, and add enough stock to bring the mixture to 8 fl oz (225 ml). Pour into a saucepan and bring to the boil.

2 Pour this hot mixture over the couscous in a large bowl, season with salt and pepper if it needs it, and mix well. Leave to steep for 10–15 minutes or until the liquid is absorbed and the couscous grains are tender. Fluff up with a fork. Whisk together all the dressing ingredients.

4 Put all the salad ingredients together in a bowl and add half the dressing. Toss together well, then add to the couscous with the remaining dressing. Toss gently to mix, then pile on to a platter and surround with the garnishes.

Roasted Buckwheat Groats (Kasha)

Kasha, an ancient and sustaining grain-like food, is not a grain at all, but a botanical fruit; the split, roasted seed of buckwheat, a flowery, distant relative of rhubarb. Kasha originated on the border between Manchuria and Russia, and has been a staple of Russian cooking for centuries. Kasha is not exactly an aristocratic food: it has an earthy, peasant quality that sustains through winters of the soul, as well as climatic winters.

Being of Russian–Jewish ancestry, I grew up with Kasha, and I still regard a warming bowlful, garnished with brown onions and sautéed mushrooms, the epitome of soul food. Plain kasha is a perfect foil for saucy vegetable stews; with the mushroom and onion garnish and a side dish of yoghurt or fromage frais and chopped herbs, it keeps the wolf from the door with a vengeance. Seek out roasted buckwheat groats in wholefood shops; if you haven't tried it before, you are in for a treat.

Basic Kasha

. . . .

Makes 1¹/₂ pints (900 ml)

2 egg whites, lightly beaten
6 oz (175 g) kasha (roasted
  buckwheat groats)

16 fl oz (475 ml) boiling stock
salt and freshly ground pepper

1 Heat a large, heavy-bottomed saucepan.

2 Stir the egg white into the kasha, mixing until the grains are well coated. Tip it into the hot pan.

3 With a wooden spoon or spatula, stir the kasha over moderate heat for about 5 minutes or until each grain is dry and separate, and the kasha smells deliciously toasty.

4 Stir the boiling stock into the kasha, season, cover and simmer over the lowest heat for 30 minutes. Remove from the heat, uncover, and drape a clean tea-towel over the open pan. Replace the lid over the tea-towel, and leave to stand for 5–10 minutes or until the liquid is absorbed and the kasha is fluffy and tender, each grain separate.

Kasha with Mushrooms and Browned Onions

. . . .

Makes 2 pints (1.1 litres)

This is a classic, but I have deconstructed it to eliminate all traces of chicken fat, and then reconstructed it with the no-fat mushroom sauté method using sherry, Teriyaki and stock. The result is a much lighter, fresher, but still deeply satisfying version of the original.

½ oz (15 g) dried mushrooms (look for cèpes or the Italian counterpart, *porcini*)

2 egg whites, lightly beaten

6 oz (175 g) kasha (roasted buckwheat groats)

1 pint (600 ml) stock

8 oz (225 g) fresh mushrooms coarsely chopped

2 fl oz (50 ml) dry sherry

generous dash of soy or Teriyaki sauce

1 mild onion, coarsely chopped

salt and freshly ground pepper

1 Rinse the dried mushrooms well under cold running water. Put them in a bowl, cover generously with hot water, and leave to soak for 20 minutes. Tip the mushrooms into a sieve lined with a double layer of coffee filter papers or muslin to strain off the soaking water. Reserve mushrooms and water. Briefly rinse the soaked mushrooms once more under cold running water. Trim off and discard any tough stems, then coarsely chop the dried mushrooms.

2 Stir the egg whites into the kasha, mixing until the grains are well coated with the egg. Heat a large, heavy-bottomed saucepan, tip in the kasha and stir with a wooden spoon or spatula over moderate heat for about 5 minutes or until each grain is dry and separate, and the kasha smells deliciously toasty. Remove from the heat.

3 Combine 8 fl oz (225 ml) of the stock with 8 fl oz (225 ml) of the reserved mushroom soaking liquid, pour into a saucepan and bring to the boil. Stir the boiling liquid into the kasha, cover the pan and simmer over the lowest heat for 30 minutes. Remove from the heat, uncover, and drape a clean tea-towel over the open pan. Replace the lid over the tea-towel and leave to stand for 5–10 minutes or until the liquid is absorbed and the kasha is fluffy and tender, with each grain separate.

4 Meanwhile, put the soaked mushrooms in a heavy-bottomed frying pan with the fresh mushrooms, 2 fl oz (50 ml) of the remaining stock, the sherry and the soy or Teriyaki sauce. Bring to the boil, then reduce the heat and simmer briskly, stirring occasionally, until the liquid is almost gone, and the mushrooms are 'frying' in their own juices. Transfer to a bowl and set aside. Wipe out the frying pan.

5 Put the onion in the frying pan with the remaining stock, cover and bring to the boil. Reduce the heat slightly and simmer briskly for 5–7 minutes. Uncover and continue cooking until the onion is meltingly tender and syrupy. Add to the mushrooms. Taste, and season with salt and pepper if necessary.

6 When the kasha is ready, combine it with the onion and the mushrooms.

NOTE

This may be prepared in advance and reheated in the microwave or conventional oven. To make the classic and beloved Russian–Jewish dish, *Kasha Varnishkas*, mix equal amounts of this kasha with freshly boiled and drained bow-tie-shaped pasta.

Millet

Millet is perhaps better known as bird food, but birds eat the unhulled variety. The hull is inedible for humans, presumably because we lack gizzards. Hulled millet, available in wholefood shops, has a delicate nut-like flavour and a pleasing chewy texture. Toasting it first in a heavy-bottomed pan brings out the delicate flavour. Like rice, millet is easier to measure out in a measuring jug.

Chinese-Style Millet and Mushrooms in Lettuce Parcels

. . . . **V** . . . .

Makes 2 pints (1.1 litres) millet and mushroom mixture

I oz (25 g) dried shiitake mushrooms (about 10)

I crisphead lettuce, such as iceberg or Webb's Wonder

½ pint (300 ml) millet

2 garlic cloves, crushed

½ inch (1 cm) piece of fresh root ginger, peeled and crushed

7 spring onions, sliced

10 fresh mushrooms, cut into quarters or eighths

2 fl oz (50 ml) dry sherry

several dashes of Teriyaki sauce

12 fl oz (350 ml) stock

salt and freshly ground pepper

juice of I lime

juice of ½ large orange

2 teaspoons sugar

8 oz (230 g) can of water chestnuts, drained and quartered

chopped fresh coriander, to taste

sliced spring onions, to serve

1 Rinse the dried mushrooms under cold running water. Put them in a bowl, cover with plenty of hot water (about 1 pint/600 ml), and leave to soak for 20 minutes.

2 Separate the leaves from the lettuce, wash well and shake dry. Trim off and discard the tough stem from each leaf. Wrap the leaves in a tea-towel and refrigerate until serving time.

3 Put the millet in a heavy-bottomed frying pan and heat gently, stirring constantly for about 3 minutes or until the grains smell beautifully toasty (not scorched) and some of them begin to pop. Tip the millet into a bowl.

4 Tip the dried mushrooms and their soaking liquid into a sieve lined with a double layer of muslin or coffee filter papers set over a bowl. Strain off the liquid. Reserve the mushrooms and the liquid. Cut the mushrooms into ½ inch (1 cm) pieces, discarding any tough stems.

5 Put *half* the soaked mushrooms in a heavy-bottomed saucepan or flameproof casserole with the garlic, ginger, spring onions, fresh mushrooms, sherry, Teriyaki sauce and 2–3 fl oz (50–75 ml) of the reserved mushroom soaking liquid. Bring to the boil, then reduce the heat and simmer, stirring occasionally, until the mushrooms are tender and most of the liquid has been absorbed.

6 Mix the stock with ½ pint (300 ml) of the remaining mushroom liquid, and add to the mushroom mixture with the millet. Season with salt and pepper. Bring to the boil, cover and simmer on the lowest heat for 20 minutes. Remove from the heat, uncover, and fluff up with a fork. Drape a clean tea-towel over the open pan. Replace the lid over the tea-towel and leave to stand for 5–10 minutes.

7 Mix the lime and orange juice with 4 fl oz (100 ml) of the remaining mushroom soaking liquid, and stir in the sugar. When the millet is ready, spoon it into a bowl. Add the lime and orange mixture, the water chestnuts, remaining soaked mushrooms, and some chopped coriander. Toss with two spoons to combine thoroughly.

8 To serve, mound the millet in the centre of a large platter. Sprinkle with spring onions and additional coriander, and surround with the lettuce leaves. To eat, spoon some of the grain on to a lettuce leaf, roll it up and eat with your fingers. Forget knives and forks for this one.

Polenta

Polenta is a kind of savoury porridge made from maize meal. It is a staple of Alpine Italy and the Swiss Ticino. It is also a staple in parts of Africa, where it is known as 'mealy-mealy'; in Rumania, where it is called 'mamaliga'; and in the southern states of America, where it bears the unlovely name 'corn meal mush'. Maize originated in the New World; it didn't reach Italy until the seventeenth century, but despite its relative youth in that part of the world, it has become a deeply entrenched staple. If you can't find quick-cooking polenta, use the ordinary kind, but cook it for 10–15 minutes longer in step 1.

Polenta and Aubergine Gratin

Serves 6

two 14 oz (400 g) cans of chopped tomatoes

1³/₄ pints (1 litre), plus 4 fl oz (100 ml) stock

6 fl oz (225 ml) quick-cooking polenta (coarse maize meal)

salt and freshly ground pepper

1 large onion, coarsely chopped

1 red or yellow pepper, peeled, deseeded and coarsely chopped

2 garlic cloves, crushed

¹/₂ teaspoon dried basil

4 fl oz (100 ml) dry red wine

4–6 ripe tomatoes, peeled, deseeded and chopped

2–3 tablespoons tomato purée

4 tablespoons chopped fresh parsley

2 medium aubergines, cut into ¹/₂ inch (1 cm) slices and grilled (see page 129)

6 tablespoons grated Parmesan cheese

1 Tip the canned tomatoes into a bowl, reserving the empty cans. Wash out the cans thoroughly and leave upside-down to drain.

2 Put the 1³/₄ pints (1 litre) stock in a large saucepan, and bring to the boil. With a wire whisk, whisk in the polenta, whisking well so the mixture does not form lumps. Bring back to the boil, then immediately lower the heat and cook over low heat, stirring with a wooden spoon, for about 5 minutes or until the polenta is smooth and very thick. As it cooks, taste, and season with salt if needed. Be careful the mixture does not scorch. Pack into the two cleaned tomato cans, cool, cover with cling film and refrigerate. Preheat the oven to 350°F, 180°C, Gas Mark 4.

3 Put the onion, red or yellow pepper, garlic, basil, wine and 100 ml (4 fl oz) stock in a saucepan, cover and bring to the boil. Reduce the heat and simmer for about 10 minutes. Uncover and continue cooking until the vegetables are tender and the liquid almost gone. Stir in the canned and fresh tomatoes and simmer for 15–20 minutes. Stir in the tomato purée and parsley, and simmer for 5 minutes more. Season with salt and pepper, remove from the heat and set aside.

4 Push or shake the polenta out of the cans (it will come out in compact cylinders). The top of each cylinder will be crusty; cut a thin slice off the top and discard. Cut the remainder into roughly ½ inch (1 cm) slices and arrange in a shallow baking dish, alternating each slice with a slice of grilled aubergine. Spread the sauce over them and sprinkle with Parmesan. Bake for 30 minutes or until hot and bubbly.

VARIATION

Grilled Polenta with Broad Bean Sweetcorn Stew

polenta, cooked and packed into cans (see step 2, above)

Broad Bean Sweetcorn Stew (see page 107)

thinly sliced half-fat mozzarella cheese

freshly ground pepper

1 Preheat the grill to its highest heat.

2 Shake the polenta 'cylinders' out of the cans. Cut a thin slice from the top of each and discard. Slice the polenta and arrange in one layer on a non-stick baking sheet. Grill, 6 inches (15 cm) from the heat, for 4–6 minutes or until beginning to brown on top.

3 Spoon a generous quantity of the stew on to each polenta round, and top with a slice of mozzarella. Sprinkle generously with freshly ground pepper. Grill, 3 inches (8 cm) from the heat for 3–5 minutes or until the cheese is melted, bubbly and speckled with brown. Lift the slices off the sheet with a spatula, and place on plates. Alternatively, the polenta rounds can be placed in a baking dish in one layer, covered with stew, and cheese slices laid on top. Grill until bubbly and lightly browned.

Savoury Polenta Pie with Garlic and Spring Onions

Makes one 8 inch (20.5 cm) pie

Try polenta cooked with spring onions, flavoured with cheese, moulded into a cake tin, and baked until the wafting fragrance drives you mad with hunger. A wedge of this is great with a steaming bowl of soup, or with some of the bean dishes or vegetable stews in other chapters of this book. This pie serves 6 people.

12 spring onions, thinly sliced

1–2 garlic cloves, finely chopped

3 pints (1.7 litres) well-seasoned stock

12½ oz (360 g) quick-cooking polenta

salt and freshly ground pepper

6 tablespoons grated Parmesan cheese

1 Preheat the oven to 350°F, 180°C, Gas Mark 4.

2 Put the spring onions, garlic and ½ pint (300 ml) of the stock in a heavy-bottomed saucepan. Cover, bring to the boil and boil for 5 minutes, then uncover, reduce the heat slightly, and simmer briskly until the onions and garlic are tender, and the liquid is almost gone.

3 Pour in the remaining stock, and bring almost to the boil. When just below boiling point, pour in the polenta in a steady stream, stirring constantly with a wire whisk. Switch from the whisk to a wooden spoon, and cook, stirring, for about 5 minutes or until the mixture is thick and smooth. (Watch out for volcanic bubbles; wear an oven glove to protect your hand and arm.) Season with salt and pepper, and stir in the Parmesan cheese.

4 Spoon and scrape the mixture into a non-stick, 8 inch (20.5 cm) diameter round cake tin with a removable bottom. Smooth the surface with the back of the spoon. Bake in the oven for 25–30 minutes or until firm and fragrant. Cool on a wire rack for 5 minutes, then loosen all around the edges and remove the sides of the tin. Cut into wedges.

Pasta

Lemony Pasta Pilaff

. . . . V . . . .

Very small pasta shapes can be cooked – like rice – by the absorption method. A good stock is imperative (see page 8 for a discussion of vegetable stocks). I make this frequently, because it's perfect after a long tiring day, when something simple, unchallenging, easy to prepare and to eat, and – most important – deeply comforting, is needed. I usually make it with tiny pasta shells, but any small pasta will do. Once, in desperation (I had run out of pasta shells), I made this with tiny dinosaur-shaped pasta I found lurking in the back of the cupboard, left over from a godson's visit. I enjoyed every swallow, although I did feel a little foolish shovelling in shoals of tyrannosaurs and brontosaurs! Serve this plain, or with a small shower of grated medium-fat cheese stirred in, or with a dollop of tomato or pepper sauce (see pages 92 and 99) ladled on top. If you want to wake up your palate, rather than lull it into gentle calm, top the hot pasta pilaff with icy Mexican Salsa (see page 187). See the note on page 50 regarding serving quantities.

I pint (600 ml) well-seasoned
stock
8 oz (225 g) mini-pasta shells
(*conchigliette rigate*)

juice of ½–I small lemon
salt and freshly ground pepper

I Put the stock in a heavy-bottomed saucepan that can be tightly covered, and bring to the boil. Stir in the pasta and the juice of ½ lemon. Season with pepper and a little salt, if necessary, and bring back to the boil. Stir once, turn the heat to low, cover the pan and simmer for 5–8 minutes or until most of the liquid has been absorbed (exact timing depends on the pan, the pasta, and your cooker).

2 Uncover the pan, stir in the juice of the second lemon half (if you wish), and remove from the heat. Drape a clean tea-towel over the open pan, replace the lid over the towel, and leave to stand for 5 minutes or until the pasta is quite tender and the liquid absorbed. It will have an almost buttery quality – consider it gastronomic emotional therapy!

Pasta with Fresh Vegetable Sauce

· · · · · · · · · · · · **V** · · · · · · · · · · · ·

Serves 2–4

*Put the water for the pasta in a large saucepan and prepare this fresh
and delicate sauce while it comes to the boil.*

6 oz (175 g) button mushrooms,
  quartered

1 bunch of spring onions, thinly
  sliced

1 garlic clove, crushed

8 fl oz (225 ml) stock

1 red and 1 yellow pepper, cut
  lengthways into their natural
  sections and deseeded

1 fennel bulb

1 medium courgette

4 fresh, ripe, flavourful tomatoes

4–5 fresh basil leaves, shredded

salt and freshly ground pepper

about 12 oz–1 lb (350–450 g)
  pasta quills (*penne*)

1 Fill a large saucepan with water for the pasta, and bring it to the boil.

2 Meanwhile, put the mushrooms, spring onions, garlic and about $^1/_4$
pint (150 ml) of the stock in a flameproof casserole. Bring to the boil,
then reduce the heat and simmer until the vegetables are tender, and
most of the liquid has cooked away.

3 Meanwhile, peel the pepper pieces with a swivel-bladed peeler, and
cut them into 1 inch (2.5 cm) squares. Trim the fennel and cut in half
lengthways and then slice. Cut the courgette into $^1/_2$ inch (1 cm) slices.

4 Add the peppers to the mushroom mixture with the remaining stock,
and cook, stirring occasionally, until the peppers are almost tender. Add
the fennel and courgettes, and cook, stirring, for a few minutes more or
until all the vegetables are tender.

5 Meanwhile, put the tomatoes in a sieve and dip them into the
boiling pasta water for 10 seconds. Refresh briefly under cold running
water, then peel, deseed and roughly dice. Add to the vegetables with
the shredded basil, and season. Cook gently until the tomatoes have
lost their shape, and the mixture is thick and savoury.

6 Cook the pasta in the boiling water until *al dente*, drain it well, then
toss it with the sauce directly in the casserole. Serve at once.

Pasta with Creamy Cauliflower Sauce

. . . .

Serves 2–4

Pasta tossed with a good tomato and cauliflower sauce, and creamy ricotta cheese makes a hearty meal. For a non-dairy version, prepare to the end of step 1, and toss the vegetable sauce with the hot pasta. In fact, the cauliflower in tomato sauce is perfectly delicious all by itself as well, without the pasta.

4–5 spring onions, sliced

2–3 dry-packed sun-dried tomatoes, chopped (use scissors)

2 black olives in brine, drained and flesh slivered off the stones

1–2 garlic cloves, crushed

8 fl oz (225 ml) stock

14 oz (400 g) can of chopped tomatoes

1 lb (500 g) carton of passata

salt and freshly ground pepper

1 cauliflower, separated into florets and steamed

12 oz–1 lb (350–450 g) pasta shapes

7 oz (200 g) ricotta cheese, at room temperature

3 tablespoons grated Parmesan cheese

2 tablespoons shredded fresh basil

1 Put the onions, sun-dried tomatoes, olive slivers, garlic and stock in a large heavy-bottomed saucepan. Bring to the boil, then reduce the heat and simmer until the onions and garlic are tender and the stock almost gone. Stir in the tomatoes and passata, season with salt and pepper, and simmer for 10 minutes more. Stir in the cauliflower and simmer for another 5–10 minutes or until the cauliflower is very tender and imbued with the taste of the sauce.

2 Meanwhile, cook the pasta in boiling water until *al dente*.

3 Put the ricotta in a large bowl, and whisk in the Parmesan. Stir the basil into the cauliflower sauce, and fold into the ricotta mixture. Drain the pasta and toss with the sauce. Serve at once.

Grilled Vegetable Lasagne

Serves 4 – 6

A soufflé-like mixture of quark and beaten egg whites takes the place of the usual high-fat white sauce in this splendid lasagne. The baking time given results in a creamy-textured layer. Cook it longer and the quark–egg layer will set – not a bad thing, but I prefer the creamy texture.

I like to use fresh lasagne sheets for this recipe. They are available from Italian delicatessens and speciality shops, and from the chill cabinets of many major supermarkets. If you can't find fresh pasta, or if you are in a hurry, use packaged dried lasagne. There is no need to cook dried lasagne first: just layer it with the other ingredients, and bake.

six 5 x 6 inch (12.5 x 15 cm) sheets of fresh lasagne

1 small aubergine, sliced and grilled (see page 124)

2 small courgettes, sliced and grilled (see page 130)

2 red or yellow peppers, grilled (see page 131)

1 pint (600 ml) tomato sauce (see pages 91–2)

1 lb (450 g) skimmed milk quark

8 oz (225 g) half-fat mozzarella cheese, drained, blotted dry and shredded

salt and freshly ground pepper

3 egg whites, beaten to firm peaks

4–5 tablespoons grated Parmesan cheese

1 Preheat the oven to 400°F, 200°C, Gas Mark 6.

2 Cook the fresh lasagne sheets according to package instructions, but undercook them slightly. Drain them, spread them out on a clean tea-towel, and blot them dry with absorbent kitchen paper.

3 Chop up the grilled vegetables with kitchen scissors, and stir them into the tomato sauce.

4 Put the quark and mozzarella cheese in a food processor. Season with salt and pepper, and process until well amalgamated. Transfer to a bowl and stir in a quarter of the beaten egg whites. Fold in the remainder.

5 Spread a thin layer of tomato sauce in the bottom of a 12 x 7 inch (30.5 x 18 cm) baking dish, and cover with a layer of three sheets of lasagne. Spread on the quark mixture and sprinkle with 2 tablespoons Parmesan. Cover with three more sheets of lasagne, spread on the remaining tomato sauce and sprinkle on the remaining cheese.

6 Cover and bake in the oven for 15 minutes. Uncover and bake for a further 15–20 minutes or until puffy and bubbling.

Macaroni with Creamy Cheese Sauce

. . . .

Serves 4–6

Macaroni cheese doesn't get any easier than this – hot pasta tossed with quark (smooth non-fat curd cheese) and grated cheese in a warm bowl. As you mix the pasta into the cheese mixture, it forms a sauce that oozes into the cavities of the pasta in a seductive manner.

I lb (450 g) pasta shells (*conchiglie*), elbow macaroni or quills (*penne*)

two 7 oz (200 g) cartons of skimmed milk quark, at room temperature

4 tablespoons grated Parmesan cheese or other medium-fat cheese

4–5 fl oz (100–150 ml) skimmed milk, at room temperature

freshly ground pepper (optional)

I Cook the pasta in boiling water until *al dente*.

2 Meanwhile, process the quark, Parmesan and skimmed milk in a food processor until very well combined. Scrape into a warm bowl.

3 Drain the pasta, and immediately toss it into the cheese mixture. Grind in some pepper, if desired, and serve at once.

Bread Puddings

Savoury bread puddings make satisfying, filling and nutritious family meals. They are not desperate measures for using up old bread, but well thought out and constructed dishes that have plenty of merit of their own (although they do – when all is said and done – use up old bread in a most efficient way).

Their ingredients can be combined hours ahead of time and then left in the fridge to soak. The more efficiently the custard soaks into the bread cubes, the better the texture, and the better the rising power of the pudding. To serve for brunch, mix the ingredients the night before; for supper, mix them in the morning. If you plan to bake the pudding immediately, be sure to mix the ingredients very well, so maximum soaking occurs.

Bread and Sweetcorn Pudding

Serves 4 – 6

5 spring onions, sliced

I fresh chilli pepper, deseeded and finely chopped

¹/₂ teaspoon ground cumin

¹/₄ pint (150 ml) stock

4 fl oz (100 ml) skimmed milk

2 tablespoons skimmed milk powder

14 oz (400 g) can of creamed sweetcorn

I egg

3 egg whites

6 oz (175 g) stale bread, cut into ¹/₂ inch (1 cm) cubes

about 12 oz (350 g) canned sweetcorn kernels, drained

4 oz (100 g) half-fat mozzarella cheese, cubed

salt and freshly ground pepper

1–2 tablespoons grated Parmesan, half-fat Cheddar or Swiss cheese

1 Preheat the oven to 350°F, 180°C, Gas Mark 4.

2 Put the spring onions, chilli and cumin in a heavy-bottomed saucepan with the stock. Bring to the boil, then reduce the heat and simmer until the onions are tender and the stock almost gone.

3 Mix the milk and skimmed milk powder, and put in a large bowl with the creamed corn, the whole egg and the egg whites. Beat well together, then stir in the bread, corn kernels, mozzarella, and the onion mixture. Season with salt and pepper, and use two spoons to toss everything together very well, so that the bread absorbs the liquid.

4 Spoon the mixture into a 10 inch (25.5 cm) diameter round ovenproof dish that is about 2 inches (5 cm) deep (or use a square casserole or a gratin dish). Bake in the oven for about 40 minutes, sprinkling on the cheese 5–10 minutes before the pie is cooked. When it is puffy, browned, and a knife inserted near the centre comes out clean, remove from the oven and serve, cut into wedges.

Bread and Caramelised Onion Pudding

Serves 4 – 6

Like French onion soup without the soup, this main-dish bread pudding combines molten cheese with shreds of caramelised onion and savoury custard-soaked chunks of bread. It rises almost like a soufflé.

I large garlic clove, halved
4 large mild onions
³/₄ pint (450 ml) stock
2 fl oz (50 ml) dry vermouth
6 oz (175 g) stale crusty French bread, cut into ¹/₂ inch (1 cm) cubes
2 eggs

2 egg whites
16 fl oz (450 ml) skimmed milk
3 tablespoons skimmed milk powder
4 tablespoons grated Parmesan or medium-fat Swiss cheese
salt and freshly ground pepper

1 Preheat the oven to 350°F, 180°C, Gas Mark 4.

2 Choose a shallow round or oval gratin dish and rub it thoroughly with the cut side of the garlic clove. Discard the garlic.

3 Cut the onions in half and slice into thin half-moons. Put the onions in a deep 10 inch (25 cm) heavy-bottomed frying pan and add the stock. Cover, bring to the boil, and boil for about 10 minutes.

4 Uncover the pan, reduce the heat, and simmer, stirring occasionally, until the onions are meltingly tender, beginning to turn amber, and the liquid is almost gone. Pour in the vermouth and simmer briskly until the liquid cooks away, stirring and scraping up any browned bits from the bottom of the pan as it simmers.

5 Toss the bread and onions together in a large bowl.

6 Beat the eggs and egg whites lightly together. Mix the milk and skimmed milk powder together, and beat into the egg mixture. Season with salt and pepper. Pour the mixture evenly over the bread and sprinkle on the grated cheese. Gently toss and mix with two spoons to saturate the bread with the egg mixture. Pour the mixture into the gratin dish.

7 Bake in the oven for 45–50 minutes or until set, puffed and golden. (A knife inserted near the centre should emerge clean.)

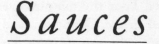

Sauces

A repertoire of basic sauces can help glamorise a bowl of pasta, a jacket potato, a bowl of mash or a plate of steamed vegetables. But a sauce should be more than decoration or fancy dressing – it should add its own good measure of nutrition as well. All of these sauces are based on vegetables, instead of on flour–fat roux, butter–egg yolk emulsions, or full-fat dairy products. And all of them (except the Colombian Tomato–Cheese Sauce) are suitable for vegans.

Top to bottom Pasta with Fresh Vegetable Sauce (page 82), Lentil 'Bolognaise' Sauce (page 97) served with spaghetti

Opposite page 91, top to bottom Tomato and Watercress Relish (page 189), Stir-Fried Peppers (page 151), Savoury Polenta Pie with Garlic and Spring Onions (page 80) on a plate with Aubergine Bean Stew (page 110)

Classic Slim Cuisine Tomato Sauce

· · · · · · · · · · · ·Ⓥ· ·Ⓩ · · · · · · · · · ·

Makes 1¹/₂ pints (900 ml)

Tomato sauce is one of the most useful of sauces, and one of the easiest as well, given the wide variety of excellent canned, bottled and 'cartoned' tomato products available in every supermarket. My basic tomato sauce, a staple in my Slim Cuisine series of books as well as in my personal cookery, is worth making in quantity and then freezing in small portions. If you plan to freeze it, omit the fresh herbs. Add them after thawing and reheating. Dried herbs can be added before freezing. The sauce is superb on pasta or pizza, or as part of countless recipes. I have one reader who spreads it on hot toast!

3 shallots, finely chopped *or* 1 mild onion, chopped

2 garlic cloves, crushed

pinch of cayenne pepper

6 fl oz (175 ml) stock

6 fl oz (175 ml) dry red wine, white wine or vermouth

1 tablespoon chopped fresh basil *or* ¹/₄ teaspoon dried basil

1 tablespoon chopped fresh thyme *or* ¹/₄ teaspoon dried thyme

1 tablespoon chopped fresh oregano *or* ¹/₄ teaspoon dried oregano

three 14 oz (400 g) cans of chopped tomatoes

salt and freshly ground pepper

2 tablespoons tomato purée

1 tablespoon chopped fresh parsley

1 Put the shallots or onion, garlic, cayenne, stock, wine and dried herbs, if using, in a heavy-bottomed frying pan. Cover, bring to the boil, and boil for 5–7 minutes. Uncover, reduce the heat and simmer briskly until the liquid has almost gone.

2 Stir in the tomatoes, and season with salt and pepper. Simmer, partially covered, for 20 minutes. Stir in the tomato purée and simmer for 10 minutes more. If you are using fresh herbs, stir them in now, including the parsley. Taste and adjust the seasonings.

Quick Tomato Sauce

· · · · · · · · · · ·(V)· ·(Z)· · · · · · · · · · · · ·

Makes 1 ¹/₂ pints (900 ml)

Passata is simply puréed, sieved tomatoes, available in cartons, cans or jars. A carton of passata, a can of tomatoes, and a garlic–olive infusion produce a spectacular tomato sauce in less than 20 minutes.

5–6 spring onions, sliced

3 black olives in brine, drained and flesh slivered off the stones

3–4 dry-packed, sun-dried tomatoes, chopped (use scissors)

1–2 garlic cloves, crushed

1–2 pinches chrushed dried chillies

1–2 pinches of dried oregano

6–8 fl oz (175–225 ml) stock

1 lb (500 g) carton of passata

14 oz (400 g) can of chopped tomatoes

freshly ground pepper

1 Put the onions, olive pieces, sun-dried tomatoes, garlic, chilli, oregano and stock in a heavy-bottomed frying pan. Cover, and bring to the boil, and boil for 3–4 minutes. Uncover, reduce the heat, and simmer until the onions and garlic are tender and the liquid has cooked down considerably and become syrupy.

2 Stir in the passata and chopped tomatoes, and grind in some pepper. Simmer briskly for 10–15 minutes or until thick and savoury. Taste and adjust the seasoning, if necessary, before serving.

Roasted Tomato Ketchup

· · · · · · · · · · · · · **V** · · **Z** · · · · · · · · · · · · · ·

Makes ³/₄ pint (450 ml)

For oven-fried potatoes (see page 175), an accompanying puddle of
tomato sauce for dabbling is a nice touch. Eating fried potatoes with
the fingers, dunking the pieces into the sauce between bites, is like
being a child again. When good tomatoes are available, char them in
the oven (or you could put them on the barbecue), then peel them and
use to make a thick, smoky purée.

15 very ripe, flavourful, juicy
  tomatoes
2 large mild onions, finely
  chopped
4 garlic cloves, crushed

4 fl oz (100 ml) red wine
3 fl oz (75 ml) stock
salt and freshly ground pepper

1 Preheat the oven to 425°F, 220°C, Gas Mark 7.

2 Put the tomatoes in one layer on a baking sheet, and bake,
uncovered, in the oven for about 30 minutes or until blistered and
charred. Leave to cool slightly.

3 While the tomatoes are baking, put the onions, garlic, wine and
stock in a heavy-bottomed frying pan. Cover, bring to the boil, and boil
for 5–7 minutes. Uncover, reduce the heat and simmer briskly until the
onions are tender and beginning to brown, and the liquid is almost
gone.

4 When the tomatoes have cooled somewhat, squeeze them out of
their skins into the frying pan. Discard the skins. Simmer the tomato
pulp for about 20 minutes or until it is thick. Season with salt and
pepper, and leave to cool slightly.

5 Pour the sauce into a blender and purée until smooth. Rub through a
sieve to eliminate the seeds.

Gravy

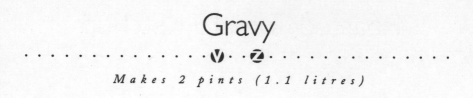

Makes 2 pints (1.1 litres)

Puréed cooked vegetables can be used to make a rich-tasting sauce, although the fat level is virtually nil. The red wine adds luxurious depth to the sauce, but it is simmered briskly so that the alcohol evaporates, leaving flavour, but no inebriating quality. Freeze the sauce in small containers, so it is available when you need it. The best way to serve gravy? Scoop a generous serving of mashed potatoes (or mashed potatoes mixed with puréed Foil-Roasted Vegetables (see page 136)) on to a plate. Make a deep dent in the mound of mash, ladle out a generous measure of gravy, and overfill the dent, so that the gravy overflows and dribbles down the sides of the mound. Surround with a moat of additional gravy. Eat with a large spoon.

4 shallots *or* I small onion, chopped
I large mild onion, chopped
2 celery stalks, chopped
2 garlic cloves, crushed
2 carrots, chopped

3 pints (1.7 litres) stock
I pint (600 ml) dry red wine
I bay leaf
14 oz (400 g) can of chopped tomatoes
salt and freshly ground pepper

1 Put the vegetables in a heavy-bottomed frying pan with ½ pint (300 ml) of the stock. Cover, bring to the boil, and boil for 5 minutes.

2 Uncover, reduce the heat slightly, and simmer, stirring occasionally, until the vegetables are tender, and the liquid almost gone.

3 Stir in the wine, bay leaf and tomatoes. Simmer briskly, uncovered, for 15 minutes.

4 Stir in the remaining stock, and simmer for 15 minutes, stirring occasionally. Remove the bay leaf and leave to cool slightly.

5 Pour into a blender and purée until smooth. Sieve into a bowl, rubbing through the solids with a wooden spoon. Season with salt and pepper and reheat gently.

Spicy Bean Sauce

· · · · · · · · · · · · · · · **V** · · **Z** · · · · · · · · · · · · · · ·

Makes 2¹/₂ pints (1.4 litres)

Lavish this lively sauce over pasta, couscous, polenta or any of your favourite grains. It's good in a rice crust, too (see page 56), with a little half-fat mozzarella melted on top.

1 large mild onion, coarsely
   chopped
2 garlic cloves, crushed
2 celery stalks, cut into ¹/₂ inch
   (1 cm) slices
1 teaspoon dried thyme
1 bay leaf
1 teaspoon dried tarragon
1 teaspoon ground cumin
pinch of cayenne pepper
¹/₂ teaspoon ground allspice

6 fl oz (175 ml) stock
2 fl oz (50 ml) red wine
2 red peppers, peeled, deseeded
   and coarsely chopped
two 14 oz (400 g) cans of
   chopped tomatoes
· 1 tablespoon drained capers
15 oz (432 g) can of red kidney,
   borlotti or pinto beans, drained
   and rinsed
salt and freshly ground pepper

1 Put the onion, garlic, celery, herbs and spices in a frying pan with the stock and red wine. Cover, bring to the boil, and boil for 5 minutes. Uncover, reduce the heat slightly, and simmer until the onion is tender.

2 Add the red peppers, stir and cook until they are softened.

3 Stir in the tomatoes and capers, and simmer, uncovered, for about 30 minutes or until thickened and savoury, stirring occasionally. Stir in the beans and season with salt and pepper. Simmer for a further 5–10 minutes. Remove the bay leaf before serving.

Herbed Aubergine Sauce

· · · · · · · · · · · · · · ·Ⓥ· · ·Ⓩ· · · · · · · · · · · · · · ·

Makes 1 pint (600 ml)

If you don't like fennel and rosemary, leave them out and replace with herbs you do like: oregano and shredded basil, thyme and bay leaf, for example. Herbed Aubergine Sauce is part-stew, part-sauce, and goes particularly well with grains like couscous or bulghur.

2 aubergines, about 8 oz (225 g) each, peeled and finely chopped

6 spring onions, chopped

2 garlic cloves, crushed

½–1 tablespoon fennel seeds

1 tablespoon rosemary leaves, crumbled

pinch of crushed dried chillies

4 fl oz (100 ml) dry red wine

about 1 pint (600 ml) stock

4 peppers (2 yellow and 2 red, if possible), peeled, deseeded and cut into thin strips

14 oz (400 g) can of chopped Italian tomatoes

1 tablespoon tomato purée

salt and freshly ground pepper

1 Put the aubergine, onions, garlic, herbs and spices, wine and ½ pint (300 ml) stock in a large, heavy-bottomed frying pan. Cover, bring to the boil, and boil for 5 minutes. Uncover, reduce the heat slightly, and simmer, stirring frequently, until the aubergine is tender and the liquid almost gone. Add more stock during the simmering, if necessary.

2 Meanwhile, put 8 fl oz (225 ml) stock and the peppers in another frying pan. Stir-'fry' until the liquid is almost gone, and the peppers are meltingly tender. Add to the aubergine mixture.

3 Stir in the tomato purée, season with salt and pepper, and simmer for 10–15 minutes or until thick and savoury. Taste and adjust the seasonings. Serve with pasta or grains, as a filling for jacket potatoes or potato cases (see pages 171, 116), or use as a filling in a vegetarian lasagne.

Lentil 'Bolognese' Sauce

· · · · · · · · · · · · · · ⓥ · · ⓩ · · · · · · · · · · · ·

Makes 2 pints (1.1 litres)

This really looks like Bolognese sauce; the lentils give it a 'meaty' texture, but it is not at all stodgy. Lentil Bolognese is perfect for pasta, but it makes a wonderful filling for Steam-Roasted Stuffed Mushrooms (see page 126), as well. I love it so much, I eat it straight out of the bowl (or the frying pan, if I just can't wait).

4 fl oz (100 ml) dry red wine

1 1/2 pints (900 ml), plus 2–3 fl oz (50–75 ml) salt-free stock or water

8 spring onions, sliced

2 dry-packed sun-dried tomatoes, chopped (use scissors)

2–3 black olives in brine, drained and flesh slivered off the stones

1–2 pinches of crushed dried chillies

1/4 teaspoon dried oregano

1–2 garlic cloves, crushed

8 oz (225 g) brown or green lentils, rinsed and picked over

two 14 oz (400 g) cans of chopped tomatoes

salt and freshly ground pepper

vegetable bouillon powder (optional)

1 Put the wine, 1/2 pint (300 ml) of the stock or water, the onions, sun-dried tomatoes, olive pieces, chilli, oregano and garlic in a heavy-bottomed saucepan or flameproof casserole. Bring to the boil, then reduce the heat and simmer until the liquid is almost gone.

2 Stir in the remaining stock or water, the lentils and canned tomatoes. Season with pepper and simmer for 45–60 minutes or until the lentils are tender and the sauce thick.

3 If you have used water instead of stock, add some vegetable bouillon powder at this point. At any rate, season with salt.

4 Ladle out about a third of the sauce and dilute it with 2–3 fl oz (50–75 ml) stock. In small batches, purée it in a blender until smooth. Combine the puréed and unpuréed sauce.

Colombian Tomato–Cheese Sauce

. . . .

Makes 1¹/₂ pints (900ml)

Papas a la Chorreadas *is a spicy Colombian dish of boiled potatoes smothered in a creamy, tomato and cheese sauce. Half-fat mozzarella is not a bad substitute for the mild white cheese of the original, and ricotta stands in for the cream. Serve with jacket potatoes or with Steam-Roasted Potatoes (see page 176).*

I large onion, chopped

2 garlic cloves, crushed

I fresh chilli, deseeded and finely chopped

¹/₂ pint (300 ml) stock

I teaspoon ground tumeric

I teaspoon ground cumin

two 14 oz (400 g) cans of tomatoes, drained and chopped

salt and freshly ground pepper

2–3 tablespoons chopped fresh coriander

6 tablespoons ricotta cheese, at room temperature

3 oz (75 g) half-fat mozzarella cheese, cut into small dice

1 Put the onion, garlic, chilli, stock and spices in a heavy-bottomed saucepan or frying pan. Cover, bring to the boil, and boil for 5–7 minutes. Uncover, reduce the heat, and simmer for 3–5 minutes or until the onions are tender, and the stock almost gone.

2 Stir in the tomatoes and simmer for 10–15 minutes or until thick. Season with salt and pepper, stir in the coriander and remove from the heat.

3 Stir a tablespoon of the sauce into the ricotta, then stir the ricotta mixture back into the sauce.

4 Stir in the mozzarella, return to the heat and allow to warm gently. (Don't simmer or the ricotta may separate; the mozzarella should just turn to meltingly soft lumps – if it melts too much, it becomes stringy.)

Red Pepper and Tomato Sauce

. . . . ⓥ . . ⓩ . . . .

Makes 1 ¹/₂ pints (900 ml)

Red peppers (and yellow ones, see the following recipe) make vivid sauces. Peppers are more digestible when peeled, and the texture is much improved, but there is no need to peel them for this sauce, because sieving the sauce in step 4 eliminates the pepper skins. If you want to make a Red Pepper Sauce (as opposed to a Red Pepper and Tomato Sauce), omit the chopped tomatoes and double the amount of peppers.

1 pint (600 ml) stock
1 large mild onion, chopped
1 garlic clove, crushed
1 tablespoon paprika
6 red peppers, deseeded and
  coarsely chopped

14 oz (400 g) can of chopped
  tomatoes
salt and freshly ground pepper

1 Put half the stock, the onion, the garlic and the paprika in a heavy-bottomed frying pan. Cover, bring to the boil, and boil for 5–7 minutes. Uncover, reduce the heat and simmer, stirring occasionally, until the onions are almost tender and the liquid almost gone.

2 Stir in the peppers and the remaining stock, and simmer, uncovered, over a moderate heat for a few minutes or until the peppers are tender and the liquid greatly reduced.

3 Add the tomatoes, season with salt and pepper, and simmer, uncovered, for 15–20 minutes or until thick and savoury. Leave to cool slightly.

4 Purée the sauce in small batches in a blender, then push the sauce through a sieve. Taste, and adjust the seasonings, if necessary.

Yellow Pepper Tarragon Sauce

· · · · · · · · · · · · · · ⓥ · ⓩ · · · · · · · · · · · · · ·

Makes ³/₄ pint (450 ml)

I first developed this tart, tarragon-infused yellow pepper sauce over 12 years ago, after losing 6 stone in weight, and pledging myself to a high-nutrition, lower-fat way of life. In those days, new as I was to the low-fat game, I wondered how I would survive without all those beloved fat- and oil-laden concoctions that made me enormous in the first place. Yellow Pepper Sauce, with a tarragon wine vinegar-flavoured base, was my variation on the theme of Béarnaise Sauce — the tarragon-infused egg yolk–butter emulsion. Over the years, my palate has learned to hate the fatty textures of egg yolk–butter emulsions, and to love the soothing smoothness of stock-sautéed vegetable purées. I never miss Béarnaise these days, but I do crave this one. Serve it with Steamed Asparagus, Vegetable-Stuffed Peppers (see page 124), or with Bean Cakes (see page 108).

6 large yellow peppers, deseeded and coarsely diced

½ pint (300 ml) stock

4 fl oz (100 ml) dry white wine or dry vermouth

2 fl oz (50 ml) tarragon wine vinegar

½ teaspoon dried tarragon, crumbled

pinch of cayenne pepper

4 spring onions, sliced

1 tablespoon chopped fresh parsley

salt and freshly ground pepper

1 Put all the ingredients in a deep, heavy-bottomed frying pan. Bring to the boil, then reduce the heat and simmer, uncovered, for 20–30 minutes or until the peppers are tender, and the liquid greatly reduced. Leave to cool slightly.

2 Purée the pepper mixture in batches in a blender, then push through a sieve, rubbing the purée through with a wooden spoon. The pepper skins will be left behind; discard them.

3 Return the sauce to the pan and bring to a simmer. Taste, and adjust the seasonings, if necessary.

Terracotta Vegetable Sauce
· · · · · · · · · · · · · **(V)** · · **(Z)** · · · · · · · · · · · ·

Makes 1 pint (600 ml)

Named for its colour, this (like the Gravy recipe on page 94) is a good example of how vegetable purées can be used to make rich no-fat sauces. Sieving only half the sauce gives an interesting texture, but sieve the whole thing if you want it totally smooth. Serve with potatoes, steamed cauliflower, pasta, or ladle it over rice or one of the alternative grains (see pages 51, 67, 69 and 73).

1 lb (450 g) mushrooms, quartered

2 onions, chopped

2 large red peppers, deseeded, peeled and chopped

2 garlic cloves, crushed

1 large carrot, coarsely grated

about 2 pints (1.1 litres) stock

$^{1}/_{4}$ pint (150 ml) dry white wine

2 dashes of Teriyaki sauce

$^{1}/_{2}$ teaspoon dried tarragon

$^{1}/_{2}$ teaspoon ground allspice

2 tablespoons tomato purée

salt and freshly ground pepper

1 Put the mushrooms, onions, peppers, garlic, carrot, $^{1}/_{2}$ pint (300 ml) stock, wine, Teriyaki sauce, tarragon and allspice in a large, heavy-bottomed frying pan. Stir to combine very well. Bring to the boil, then reduce the heat slightly and simmer briskly until the vegetables are tender and the liquid is greatly reduced and syrupy. Lower the heat and let the vegetables gently 'fry' in their own juices for a few minutes, stirring occasionally.

2 Stir in the tomato purée, season with salt and pepper, and leave to cool slightly.

3 Purée the mixture, in small batches, in a blender or food processor until smooth. Push half the purée through a sieve, then mix the sieved sauce with the unsieved sauce. Leave to cool completely, then cover and refrigerate until needed.

4 To reheat, pour into a saucepan and thin, if necessary, with 2–3 tablespoons stock or water. Simmer gently, stirring occasionally.

Beans and Pulses

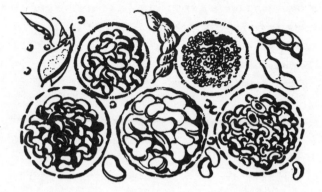

Due to their high protein count, and their substantial, filling nature, dried beans and pulses are a vegetarian staple. Although the protein they provide is not quite complete, it is complemented by grains or animal protein (in dairy products) to give a full measure of amino acids (the building blocks of protein). But it is not merely a question of impeccable nutritional references; beans make very good eating. There is an overwhelming variety to choose from, and countless ways of preparing them, so you should never have to suffer bean boredom. And – good news for the chronically rushed – more and more different types of beans are becoming available in cans, so soaking and long simmering are not always necessary. Beans do have a reputation for windiness, but, happily, the more beans you eat, the less you will suffer from this particular affliction!

Curried Kidney Beans

· · · · · · · · · · · · · **V** · · **Z** · · · · · · · · · · · · · ·

Makes 2 pints (1.1 litres)

This recipe is based on traditional Indian home cooking. Serve with Sweet Rice Pulao (see page 60) and Raita (see pages 191–2), or if time is at a minimum, with plain rice.

I large mild onion, coarsely
  chopped
³/₄ pint (450 ml) stock
¹/₂ inch (I cm) piece of fresh root
  ginger, peeled and crushed
¹/₂ teaspoon each of ground
  cinnamon, ground coriander
  and ground cumin
pinch of ground cloves
pinch of cayenne pepper

I bay leaf
I garlic clove, crushed
two I4 oz (400 g) cans of
  tomatoes, drained
two I5 oz (432 g) cans of kidney
  beans, drained and rinsed
salt
chopped fresh coriander to
  garnish

I Put the onion, ¹/₂ pint (300 ml) stock, the ginger, spices, bay leaf and garlic in a heavy-bottomed frying pan. Cover, bring to the boil, and boil for 5–7 minutes. Uncover, reduce the heat, and simmer until the onions are tender and the onions and spices are 'frying' in their own juices.

2 Crush the tomatoes with your hands and add them, with the juice from the cans, to the onions. Simmer for 3–4 minutes, then add the beans and remaining stock. Season with salt and simmer briskly for 15–20 minutes or until thick and savoury. Taste, and adjust the seasonings if necessary. Discard the bay leaf, and serve garnished with chopped coriander.

Red Beans and Rice

· · · · · · · · · · · · ·V· ·Z· · · · · · · · · · · ·

Makes 2 pints (1.1 litres)

It is said that Louis Armstrong (Satchmo) loved the classic New Orleans (excuse me, 'N'Awlins') combination of red beans and rice so much that he signed his letters 'Red Beans and Ricely Yours'. Because I dote on brown rice (and its nutritional profile is so high) I always serve these beans with the brown stuff, but white is more traditional.

1 large mild onion, coarsely chopped

2 red peppers, peeled, deseeded and coarsely chopped

2 celery stalks, chopped

1/4 teaspoon ground cumin

1/4 teaspoon ground coriander

pinch of cayenne pepper

1/4 teaspoon dried thyme

1/4 teaspoon dried oregano, crumbled

4 fl oz (100 ml) red wine

3/4 pint (450 ml) stock

14 oz (400 g) can of chopped tomatoes

1 bay leaf

salt and freshly ground pepper

two 15 oz (432 g) cans of red kidney beans, drained and rinsed

cooked rice (see page 51), to serve

1 Put the vegetables, spices, herbs, wine and stock in a heavy-bottomed frying pan. Cover, bring to the boil, and boil for 5–7 minutes. Uncover, reduce the heat, and simmer until the vegetables are nearly tender, and are 'frying' in their own juices.

2 Stir in the tomatoes and bay leaf. Season with salt and pepper, and simmer for 5 minutes.

3 Stir in the beans and simmer for 10 minutes more, or until the mixture is thick and savoury. Discard the bay leaf, and serve with rice.

Zesty Beans

. . . . **V** . . **Z** . . . .

Makes 1 1/4 pints (750 ml)

These are zesty, yet delicate. If you prefer less zest and more delicacy, leave out the chilli and chilli powder.

1 large mild onion, chopped

2 garlic cloves, crushed

1 fresh chilli, deseeded and chopped

1/2 teaspoon dried oregano, crumbled

1/2 teaspoon chilli powder

3/4 teaspoon ground cumin

1/2 pint (300 ml) stock

1 teaspoon Dijon mustard

15 oz (432 g) can of cannellini beans, drained and rinsed

15 oz (432 g) can of *haricot blancs*, drained and rinsed

14 oz (400 g) can of chopped tomatoes

2 tablespoons chopped fresh parsley

salt

chopped fresh coriander, to garnish

1 Put the onion, garlic, chilli, herbs and spices in a large frying pan with the stock. Cover, bring to the boil, and boil for 5–7 minutes. Uncover, reduce the heat, and simmer until the onions are 'frying' in their own juices.

2 Stir in the mustard, beans, tomatoes and parsley. Season with salt, and simmer gently, stirring occasionally, for 15–20 minutes or until thick. Serve with rice or other grains, or on toast, sprinkled with chopped coriander.

Beans on Toast

· · · · · · · · · · · · · · ·**V**· ·**Z**· · · · · · · · · · · · · · ·

Makes 1¹/₄ pints (750 ml)

Of course, you could always open a can of baked beans, and throw the contents at a slice of toast, but this is almost as quick, yet it has quite a bit of pizzazz. I firmly believe that pizzazz is important, even on fraught days that leave no time or strength for serious cooking. Another soy-bean-based product, hoisin sauce is now available in most larger supermarkets.

I garlic clove, crushed

I small onion, chopped

2–3 dry-packed sun-dried tomatoes, finely chopped (use scissors) (optional)

pinch of crushed dried chillies

8 fl oz (225 ml) stock

two 15 oz (432 g) cans of black-eyed beans, broad beans, red kidney beans or borlotti beans, drained and rinsed

1–2 tablespoons spicy ketchup (such as Salsa Ketchup or Italian Ketchup)

¹/₂ pint (300 ml) passata

I tablespoon hoisin sauce

juice of ¹/₂ lime

toasted wholemeal bread

1 Put the garlic, onion, sun-dried tomatoes (if using), chilli flakes and stock in a heavy-bottomed frying pan. Cover, bring to the boil, and boil for 7–10 minutes. Uncover, and simmer briskly until the onions and garlic are tender and the liquid has almost boiled away.

2 Add the beans and stir so they are thoroughly mixed with the onion mixture. Stir the remaining ingredients (except the lime juice and toast) into the beans, and simmer for 10–15 minutes, stirring in the lime juice 5 minutes before the end of the cooking time. Ladle over toasted wholemeal bread to serve.

Broad Bean Sweetcorn Stew

· · · · · · · · · · · · ·  · · · · · · · · · · · · ·

Makes 1 ¹/₂ pints (900 ml)

Store-cupboard recipes are marvellous for those exhausted weekday evenings when you want something hot and sustaining, but have very little patience for real cooking. All you have to do here is open a few cans and chop a few herbs. Beans and corn are a time-honoured vegetarian partnership.

6 spring onions, thinly sliced

3–4 dry-packed sun-dried tomatoes, diced (use scissors) (optional)

about ¹/₂ pint (300 ml) stock

14 oz (400 g) can of baby broad beans, drained

12 oz (350 g) can of sweetcorn kernels, drained

14 oz (400 g) can of chopped tomatoes

salt and freshly ground pepper

6–7 tablespoons shredded fresh mint or basil

8 fl oz (225 ml) no-fat fromage frais

1 Put the onions, sun-dried tomatoes (if using) and stock in a heavy-bottomed frying pan. Bring to the boil, then reduce the heat and simmer until the onions and tomatoes are tender.

2 Stir in the broad beans, corn and tomatoes. Season with salt and pepper, and simmer, uncovered, for about 10 minutes, then stir in 4 tablespoons of the mint. Stir the remaining mint or basil into the fromage frais. Garnish each bowlful of stew with a dollop of the herbed fromage frais, and serve the remainder separately in a bowl.

V Omit the fromage frais garnish

Bean Cakes

Z

Makes about 8 cakes

I hate lumpy beanburgers, the kind that have bits of unmashed beans mixed in with the mashed ones. These smooth bean cakes are much more sophisticated; I especially like the contrast of the creamy bean–aubergine interior with the crisp crumb–cheese exterior. The aubergine, sponge-like, soaks up the flavours of the infusion, so that the entire bean cake is imbued with the mellow flavours of garlic and olives. Serve the cakes on one of the tomato or pepper sauces or Gravy (see pages 91–4), or accompany with Fruit–Fennel Chutney (see page 190), Mint–Coriander Raita (see page 191) or Green Pea Dip (see page 37). The bean cakes are also delicious in pita pockets, or wrapped in tortillas, garnished with the accompaniments.

INFUSION

5 spring onions, sliced

2 dry-packed sun-dried tomatoes, diced (use scissors)

3 black olives in brine, drained and flesh slivered off the stones

1/4 teaspoon dried oregano

4 oz (100 g) peeled aubergine, diced

pinch of dried chilli flakes

1–2 garlic cloves, crushed

1/2 pint (300 ml) stock

BEAN MIX

15 oz (432 g) can of borlotti or butter beans, drained and rinsed

1 tablespoon each of tomato purée, fromage frais, grated Parmesan cheese and plain breadcrumbs

salt and freshly ground pepper (optional)

COATING

5 tablespoons plain breadcrumbs

2–3 tablespoons grated Parmesan cheese

salt and freshly ground pepper

olive oil and water spray (see page 5)

1 Preheat the oven to 400°F, 200°C, Gas Mark 6.

2 Put all the infusion ingredients in a saucepan. Bring to the boil, then reduce the heat and simmer until the aubergine is very tender and the liquid has been absorbed. Leave to cool.

3 Put the cooled infusion in a food processor and add the bean mix ingredients, except the salt and pepper. Process until smooth, then taste and season with salt and pepper, if necessary.

4 For the coating, mix the plain breadcrumbs with the Parmesan cheese. Season with salt and pepper, and spread on a plate. Scoop up a heaped tablespoon of the bean mixture, form it into a rough ball, and toss it in the crumbs until evenly coated. Flatten it to ½ inch (1 cm) thick cake. Place on a non-stick baking sheet that you have lightly misted with olive oil spray. Repeat until all the bean mixture has been used.

5 Bake in the oven for 10–12 minutes, then carefully turn the cakes and bake for a further 10–12 minutes or until they are crusty and golden all over.

Aubergine Bean Stew

· · · · · · · · · · **V** · · **Z** · · · · · · · · · ·

Makes 2 pints (1.1 litres)

This is another recipe combining those natural partners, aubergines and beans, this time in a Sicilian-influenced stew. I love this ladled generously over wedges of Savoury Polenta Pie with Garlic and Spring Onions (see page 80). Of course, polenta is typical of northern Italy, far from Sicily, both culturally and geographically, but they do go together so well. Throw gastronomic cultural correctness to the winds, and enjoy it.

4–5 black olives in brine, drained and flesh slivered off the stones

2 tablespoons drained capers

1–2 tablespoons raisins

2 dry-packed sun-dried tomatoes, diced (use scissors)

3–4 garlic cloves, crushed

4 spring onions, sliced

1–2 good pinches of crushed dried chillies

½ pint (300 ml) stock

¼ pint (150 ml) dry red wine

1 aubergine, about 12 oz (350 g), peeled and diced

3 small courgettes, diced

two 14 oz (400 g) cans of tomatoes, drained and cut into strips

salt and freshly ground pepper

15 oz (432 g) can of borlotti beans, drained and rinsed

2–3 tablespoons shredded fresh basil

4–5 tablespoons chopped fresh parsley

1 Put the olive pieces, capers, raisins, sun-dried tomatoes, garlic, onions, chillies, stock and wine in a large, non-reactive flameproof casserole or heavy-bottomed saucepan. Cover, bring to the boil, and boil for 5–7 minutes.

2 Add the aubergine, courgettes and tomato strips, and season with salt and pepper. Simmer, uncovered, for 10–15 minutes, then stir in the beans and herbs, and simmer, stirring occasionally, for 5–10 minutes more or until the aubergine is tender.

Black Beans

· · · · · · · · · · · · V · · Z · · · · · · · · · · · ·

Makes 2¹/₂ pints (1.4 litres)

Black beans, also known as turtle beans, are not available already soaked and cooked in cans, so you have to do all the preliminary work yourself. It's worth it – the turtle bean is a noble bean. The colour is purple-black, the texture is velvety. Serve them as they are, with Mint and Coriander Raita (see page 191) and Mexican Salsa (see page 186), or layer them with tomato sauce (see pages 91–2) and tortilla chips (see page 47), top with shredded half-fat mozzarella, and bake. If you wish, purée half the beans and mix with the unpuréed portion for an interesting texture. These beans also form the basis of Black Bean Soup (see page 13), or – with white rice – the Cuban dish, Moors and Christians.

1 lb (450 g) dried black beans, washed and picked over

3¹/₄ pints (1.9 litres) water (if your water is very hard, use bottled water)

1 large mild onion, chopped

3³/₄ pints (2.2 litres) salt-free stock

2–4 garlic cloves, crushed

¹/₂ teaspoon ground cumin

pinch of ground cloves

¹/₄ teaspoon ground allspice

¹/₂ teaspoon ground coriander

1–2 pinches of cayenne pepper

salt and freshly ground pepper

1 Put the beans in a large bowl, pour over the water, and leave to soak overnight in a cool place. Next day, drain them, discarding the water.

2 Put the onion, ¹/₂ pint (300 ml) salt-free stock, the garlic and all the spices in a heavy-bottomed saucepan. Cover, bring to the boil, and boil for 5–7 minutes. Uncover, reduce the heat, and simmer, stirring occasionally, until the onions and spices are 'frying' in their own juices. When the onions are tender, stir in the drained beans.

3 Stir in the remaining 3¹/₄ pints (1.9 litres) salt-free stock, cover and boil hard for 10 minutes. Skim off the foam, then reduce the heat and simmer, partially covered, for 1¹/₂ hours.

4 Season with salt and pepper and simmer for a further 1 hour or until very tender. Taste and adjust the seasonings.

Puy Lentils

· · · · · · · · · · · ·**Ⓥ** · ·**Ⓩ** · · · · · · · · · · ·

Makes 1¼ pints (750 ml)

Tiny Puy lentils are suddenly very fashionable, which is fine with me; the more fashionable they become, the easier they are to find in supermarkets and wholefood shops. Puy lentils cook very quickly and have an earthy taste, as do all lentils, but with the Puy, it is a delicate earthiness, if you can imagine such a thing. I'm always delighted when a truly useful, basic and healthful food hits 'fad' status. Like sun-dried tomatoes, Puy lentils deserve their current popularity, and – like sun-dried tomatoes – I hope they are here to stay.

about 2½ pints (1.4 litres) salt-free stock or water

2 dry-packed sun-dried tomatoes, chopped (use scissors)

2 garlic cloves, crushed

6 spring onions, sliced

pinch of crushed dried chillies

3 black olives in brine, drained and flesh slivered off the stones

9 oz (250 g) Puy lentils, rinsed

freshly ground pepper

salt and vegetable bouillon powder (optional)

1 Put ¼ pint (150 ml) stock or water in a heavy-bottomed saucepan with the tomatoes, garlic, spring onions, chilli and olive pieces. Bring to the boil, then reduce the heat and simmer until the liquid is almost gone.

2 Stir in the lentils and season with pepper. Stir in 2 pints (1.1 litres) of the remaining stock, bring to the boil, and boil for 10 minutes. Reduce the heat and simmer, partially covered, for 30–35 minutes or until the lentils are tender. Add a bit more salt-free stock or water during this time, if necessary, to prevent scorching. If you have used water instead of salt-free stock, add some vegetable bouillon powder and salt.

HOW TO LOVE YOUR LIVER

If these lentils are cooled, and then puréed in a food processor, they look startlingly like liver pâté. It spreads like liver pâté too, but the taste is pure, earthy Puy lentils. Quite wonderful, really.

Green Split Pea Dhal

· · · · · · · · · · · · **Ⓥ** · · **Ⓩ** · · · · · · · · · · · ·

Makes 1³/₄ pints (1 litre)

A dhal is a kind of sauce made from cooked pulses, meant to accompany curry dishes. Serve this – along with chutneys and Raita (see pages 191–2) – with any of the vegetable curries and Sweet Rice Pulao (see page 60). The combination of tastes and textures, as well as excellent nutrition, makes a meal that is hard to beat.

1½ pints (900 ml) salt-free stock or water

½ inch (1 cm) piece of root ginger, peeled and grated

2 small onions, diced

2 garlic cloves, crushed

1 fresh green chilli, deseeded and finely chopped

1½ teaspoons ground turmeric

1½ teaspoons ground coriander

1 teaspoon ground cumin

1 teaspoon mustard powder

14 oz (400 g) can of tomatoes, drained and chopped

8 oz (225 g) dried green split peas, rinsed and picked over

salt

1 teaspoon garam masala

1 Put ½ pint (300 ml) salt-free stock or water in a heavy-bottomed saucepan with the ginger, onions, garlic, chilli and spices. Cover, bring to the boil, and boil for 5–7 minutes. Uncover, reduce the heat, and simmer, stirring occasionally, until the onions are tender, and the onions and spices are 'frying' in their own juices.

2 Stir in the tomatoes and cook for 1 minute. Stir in the split peas and remaining stock or water, and simmer, covered, for 35–45 minutes or until the peas are tender and the consistency is that of a thick sauce. Season with salt (and some vegetable bouillon powder, if you have used water instead of salt-free stock) during the last 10–15 minutes of cooking.

3 When the peas are done, stir in the garam masala. This dhal reheats well, but it will have thickened. Thin with stock or water as necessary.

Vegetables

An inspiring, life-enhancing selection of vegetables should be the heart of *any* healthy diet, not just a vegetarian one. Wander up and down the greengrocery section of your local supermarket and revel in the bounty: glossy purple aubergines; jewel-like red, yellow and orange peppers; huge posies of cauliflower curving out of their greens like virginal bouquets for vegetarian brides; sweet potatoes, salad potatoes, baking potatoes, all-purpose potatoes – an orgy of starchy comfort, all labelled to explain their purpose; thorny artichokes; thrusting asparagus; tomatoes that may actually taste like tomatoes; cabbages of all hues, curly and straight . . . it drives one wild with meal possibilities! And it's not just the sheer gastronomic joy of all this vegetable overflow; the health benefits cannot be overstated. Vegetables are *profoundly* important to your general health and well-being.

Vegetables high in beta-carotene (your body uses beta-carotene to make vitamin A) are believed to give protection against the development of cancers affecting the skin and lining tissues (such as lung and breast cancers), bladder and digestive-tract cancers, and prostate and cervical cancers. Such vegetables include asparagus, beetroot, broccoli, carrots, red and yellow peppers, dark green leaves (such as spinach, chard and watercress), tomatoes and sweetcorn.

Another vegetable group believed to protect against cancer is the brassica (cabbage) family, including Brussels sprouts, all cabbages, cauliflower, broccoli and kohlrabi. Large and frequent servings may help reduce the risk of cancers of the stomach and large intestine.

Virtually all vegetables are bursting with important vitamins and fibre, they fill you up, they keep your digestive system working nicely, and they provide much pleasure. Snack on them, dine on them, eat as many different kinds, in as many combinations, as you can. If you have little time for peeling, scraping, slicing and dicing, try frozen vegetables – they are at least as nutritious as fresh (unless you are in the habit of yanking them out of the soil and cooking them on the spot – *nothing* compares to that!).

Stuffed Stuff

Filled vegetable cases make a wonderful focus for a meal. Served with a sauce (present them on a bed of sauce, rather than smothered with it) and a salad or interesting side vegetable, they are filling, satisfying and attractive. All sorts of vegetables can be stuffed: potatoes, cabbage leaves, winter squash, courgettes: let your imagination be your guide. The following recipes and techniques should get you started in the stuffing game – multiply or divide the recipes to suit the number of those you are feeding, and their appetites.

Potato Cases

. . . . **V** . . . .

These potato skins turn crunchy, like crisps, and are meant to be filled with something wonderful; mushroom ragout, vegetable curry or chilli, lentil bolognese, or even mashed potatoes (cook the scooped out centres, mash with a dab of fromage frais and grated medium-fat cheese, and use to fill the cases).

large baking potatoes

1 Preheat the oven to 400°F, 200°C, Gas Mark 6.

2 Scrub the potatoes, and halve them lengthways.

3 With a teaspoon or melon baller, scoop out the insides of the potatoes, leaving a shell about ¼ inch (5 mm) thick. Save the scraps for another use (see box).

4 Bake directly on the oven shelf for 25–35 minutes or until golden brown and very crisp. Serve at once, filled with a savoury mixture (see above).

POTATO GRATIN

Don't throw the potato insides away. Use them to make a starchy and satisfying gratin:

1 Scoop the insides of the potatoes straight into a saucepan and add enough stock to cover. Season with salt and plenty of pepper, and a little grated nutmeg or a pinch each of ground cumin and cayenne pepper. Bring to the boil, then reduce the heat and simmer, covered, until the potato is tender. Do not drain.

2 Mash roughly (just to break up the pieces, not to purée them) in the saucepan with a potato masher, then spread in a gratin dish. Dribble on a little skimmed milk and sprinkle with some grated Parmesan or medium-fat Cheddar or Swiss cheese. Flash under the grill until bubbly and well browned on top.

Squash Cases

Acorn squash and butternut squash, two of the hard-shelled 'winter squashes', are now available during the autumn months in many supermarkets. Butternut squash has a butterscotch-coloured shell and is shaped like a gourd; acorn squash is round, ribbed, and green with orange highlights. Both, when baked, have sweet, tender, mouthfilling flesh and make excellent cases for all sorts of rice dishes or bean- and vegetable-based purées and stews. A butternut squash has a small cavity, while an acorn squash has a large one.

To bake either of the squashes, preheat the oven to 400°F, 200°C, Gas Mark 6. Halve them from stem to stern, and scrape out the seeds and fibres. Place the pieces, cavity-up, on a baking sheet, and mist lightly with oil and water spray (see page 5). Bake in the oven for 35–45 minutes (the timing depends on the size of the squash). The idea is to bake them long enough for the flesh to become very tender, but not so long that the squash halves lose their shape and collapse. Fill the cavity with any rice or vegetable mixture you like. The gorgeous yellow/orange flesh of butternut squash, and its voluptuous texture and sweet flavour, work particularly well with Sweet Rice Pulao (see page 60). Serve the rice-stuffed squash on a bed of Pepper Sauce (see page 99) or surrounded by a wreath of Stir-Fried Peppers (see page 151). Mushroom Ragout (see page 167) is especially good heaped to overflowing in a baked acorn squash half. The vegetable curry mixtures (see pages 158–162) are also very good in both squashes.

Cabbage Parcels

· · · · · · · · · · · **V** · · · · · · · · · ·

Makes 12 – 15

This is easy to make, but it is fairly labour-intensive – all that peeling, chopping, dicing, steaming and rolling. For those who enjoy kitchen activity, the preparation is as pleasurable as the eating; those in a constant rush will – no doubt – recoil in horror. These Cabbage Parcels can be made a day or so in advance – indeed the flavour improves after a day or two.

1 large Savoy cabbage
2 courgettes, 4 oz (100 g) each, chopped
1 aubergine, 6 oz (175 g), peeled and chopped
2 large carrots, chopped
2 peppers (1 red, 1 yellow), peeled, deseeded and chopped
8 spring onions, sliced
2 garlic cloves, crushed
1 tablespoon paprika
³/₄ pint (450 ml) stock

3 dry-packed sun-dried tomatoes, chopped (use scissors)
pinch of crushed dried chillies
3 black olives in brine, drained and flesh slivered off the stones
4 fl oz (100 ml) dry red wine
1 tablespoon tomato purée
6 tablespoons chopped fresh parsley
salt and freshly ground pepper
1 lb (500 g) carton of passata

1 Cut the core out of the cabbage. Remove the tough outer leaves (save them for garnish), and pull of 12–15 leaves (you will have some bigger and some smaller ones – that's fine). Set aside the heart of the cabbage. With a sharp paring knife, pare down the tough central vein on each leaf. Steam the leaves over boiling water for 5–7 minutes or until they are flexible and almost tender. Refresh under cold running water to stop further cooking, drain well, and set aside. Chop up the cabbage heart, and set aside.

2 Preheat the oven to 400°F, 200°C, Gas Mark 6.

3 Put the courgettes, aubergine, carrots, peppers, onions, garlic, paprika, ¹/₂ pint (300 ml) of the stock, the sun-dried tomatoes, chilli, olive pieces and red wine in a large, heavy-bottomed frying pan. Cover, bring to the boil, and boil for 5–7 minutes. Uncover, reduce the heat and simmer for 5–10 minutes more or until the vegetables are tender and the liquid is almost gone. Stir in the tomato purée and 4 tablespoons chopped parsley, and season with salt and pepper. Leave to cool.

4 Put a large plate on your work surface. Lay a cabbage leaf out flat on your work surface. Put 1–2 tablespoons of the vegetable mixture on one end of the leaf. Tuck in the end and the sides, and roll to make a neat parcel. Place, seam-side down, on the plate. Repeat until all the leaves are filled. There will be some leftover filling; set it aside.

5 Combine the chopped cabbage heart and remaining ¼ pint (150 ml) stock in a frying pan. Stir-fry until the cabbage is tender and the liquid almost gone. Stir in the leftover vegetable stuffing, the passata and remaining parsley. Simmer for 5 minutes, then season with salt and pepper.

6 Choose a baking dish that will hold the cabbage parcels in one snug layer. Spoon some sauce on to the bottom of the dish, then carefully arrange the cabbage rolls in the dish, seam-side down. Pour the remaining sauce over the parcels. Cover the dish and bake in the oven for 30–40 minutes or until hot and bubbling.

7 To serve, line a platter with the reserved outer cabbage leaves. Lift out the cabbage rolls (gently shaking off the sauce) and place on the leaves. Pour the sauce into a sauceboat and serve separately. Serve with mashed potatoes, kasha (see page 73) or couscous (see page 69).

Stuffed Aubergine

V · Z

Makes 2 stuffed halves

I use chopped, flat, open mushrooms to stuff aubergine halves, because they result in a dark stuffing. The almost-black mushroom stuffing contained in the dark purple aubergine case, set against the scarlet sauce, is a dramatic sight. It tastes good, too. Serve one or two halves per person.

1 aubergine, 10–12 oz (275–350 g)
oil and water spray (see page 5)
1 garlic clove, crushed
4 oz (100 g) flat mushrooms, finely chopped
4 fl oz (100 ml) red wine

2 fl oz (50 ml) stock
3 tablespoons chopped fresh parsley
salt and freshly ground pepper
Tomato or Red Pepper Sauce (see pages 91–92 and 99), to serve

1 Preheat the oven to 450°F, 230°C, Gas Mark 8.

2 Trim the stem from the aubergine and cut the aubergine in half lengthways. With a sharp knife, cut all around each aubergine half, about ¼ inch (5 mm) in from the edge. Cut almost down to the skin, but be careful not to cut through the skin. Mist the cut surfaces of the aubergine with oil spray.

3 Choose a baking dish that will hold the aubergine halves side by side. Put a few spoonfuls of water in the dish and place the aubergine halves in it, cut-sides down. Bake in the oven for 10–15 minutes or until the aubergine is partially tender. Cool slightly.

4 With a small, sharp knife, cut out the flesh from each aubergine half, leaving a shell of about ¼ inch (5 mm) thickness. The shell will most likely lie flat rather than boat-shaped; don't worry.

5 Chop the aubergine flesh and combine it, in a heavy-bottomed frying pan, with the garlic, mushrooms, wine and stock. Sauté, stirring occasionally, until the mixture is very dark, the liquid almost gone, and the mushrooms tender. Stir in 2 tablespoons chopped parsley and season with salt and pepper.

6 Spoon the mushroom mixture in a strip down the centre of each aubergine shell. Mould the shell around the filling into a boat shape. Lightly mist with oil and water spray a baking dish that will hold the stuffed shells snugly. Put the stuffed aubergines in the dish and bake, uncovered in the oven, for 15–20 minutes or until sizzling and heated through. Serve on a bed of Quick Tomato or Red Pepper Sauce. Sprinkle with the remaining chopped parsley.

GARLIC TIP

To remove the smell of raw garlic from your fingers, wash your hands first, then rub your fingers against the bowl of a stainless-steel spoon, under cold running water. Wash your hands once more and the smell will be gone.

Stuffed Courgettes

Makes 4 stuffed halves

Courgettes seem to be made for stuffing; hollowed out they form perfect little boat shapes. The chopped-up courgette flesh marries well with Italian seasonings.

2 medium courgettes
1 small onion, chopped
1 garlic clove, crushed
2 dry-packed sun-dried tomatoes, chopped (use scissors)
2 black olives in brine, drained and flesh slivered off the stones
pinch of crushed dried chillies
1/4–1/2 pint (150–300 ml) stock
2 fl oz (50 ml) dry vermouth
4 tablespoons cooked brown rice (see page 51)

freshly ground pepper
2–3 tablespoons grated Parmesan cheese
2 tablespoons chopped fresh parsley
2 tablespoons shredded fresh basil or mint
olive oil and water spray (see page 5)
lemon wedges or Red Pepper or Quick Tomato Sauce (see pages 99 and 91–92), to serve

1 Preheat the oven to 450°F, 230°C, Gas Mark 8.

2 Trim the courgettes and halve lengthways. With a teaspoon, hollow out each half, leaving a shell about 1/2 inch (1 cm) thick. Chop the scooped-out flesh, and put in a heavy-bottomed frying pan with the onion, garlic, sun-dried tomatoes, olive pieces, chilli, 1/4 pint (150 ml) stock and vermouth. Bring to the boil, and boil uncovered, for 5–7 minutes, stirring occasionally until the onions are tender and the liquid almost gone. Stir in the rice and a spoonful or so of extra stock, if necessary. Season with pepper and stir until everything is well combined and the rice is imbued with the taste of the onion–garlic mixture. Remove from the heat, and stir in most of the cheese and the herbs.

3 While the filling is cooking, steam the courgette shells over boiling water for 3–5 minutes or until *barely* tender. Refresh under cold running water to stop further cooking and set the colour. Dry with absorbent kitchen paper.

4 Choose a baking dish that will hold the courgettes in one layer, and mist it with oil and water spray. Heap the rice mixture into the courgette halves and arrange them in a baking dish. Sprinkle each with a little of the remaining cheese and bake in the oven for 15–20 minutes or until they are sizzling and the cheese has melted. Serve at once, with lemon wedges or on a bed of Red Pepper or Tomato Sauce.

Vegetable-Stuffed Peppers

· · · · · · · · · · · · · · · ·Ⓥ· ·Ⓩ· · · · · · · · · · · · · · · · · ·

Makes 6 halves

Vegetarian dishes are either very brown (all those grains and beans) or intoxicatingly colourful (all those gorgeous vegetables). The most gorgeous of them all, of course, is the pepper, and here it is used to advantage. Stuff red peppers with a colourful mixture of gently curried shredded roots and set them on a purée of yellow peppers. Edible technicolour is the result.

3 red peppers
several dashes of Teriyaki sauce
4 fl oz (100 ml), plus 2–3 tablespoons, stock
4 fl oz (100 ml) dry sherry
2 carrots, coarsely grated
2 small white turnips, grated
2 small parsnips, grated
2 tablespoons sultanas
¹/₄ teaspoon each of garam masala, ground cumin and ground turmeric

6 tablespoons cooked brown rice (see page 51)
salt and freshly ground pepper
Yellow Pepper Sauce (follow the recipe on page 100 but omit the tarragon and use plain wine vinegar), to serve
chopped fresh parsley and coriander, to garnish

1 Preheat the oven to 350°F, 180°C, Gas Mark 4.

2 Halve the peppers and remove the seeds, ribs and stems. With a swivel-bladed peeler, carefully peel each half. Steam over boiling water for 5–7 minutes or until 'crisp-tender'. Refresh under cold running water to prevent further cooking, and blot dry with absorbent kitchen paper.

3 Put the Teriyaki sauce, 4 fl oz (100 ml) of stock, the sherry, grated vegetables, sultanas and spices in a heavy-bottomed frying pan. Cook gently, stirring and tossing the vegetables until they are tender but not at all mushy, and the liquid is almost gone. Stir in the rice and season with salt and pepper.

4 Pour 2–3 tablespoons stock into a baking dish that will hold the pepper halves in one layer. Arrange the peppers in the dish, cut-sides up. Spoon the vegetable mixture into the peppers. Cover the dish and bake in the oven for 30 minutes.

5 To serve, set the pepper halves on a bed of Yellow Pepper Sauce, and sprinkle with the fresh herbs.

Steam-Roasted Stuffed Mushrooms

· · · · · · · · · Z · · · · · · · · ·

Large fresh mushrooms, stuffed or unstuffed, can be wrapped in baking parchment and roasted in a hot oven. As they roast, steam forms in the parchment parcel (it puffs up dramatically) and the mushrooms take on a succulent texture. The first time you try this should be a trial run to test your oven's performance: make a note of the baking time so that you do not have to guess next time.

large flat mushrooms
salt and freshly ground pepper
grated Parmesan cheese (optional)
olive oil and water spray (see page 5)

FILLING

Lentil 'Bolognese' Sauce (see page 97)
Rice with Spring Onions and Vermouth (see page 55)
Spicy Bean Dip (see page 42)
Spinach Filling (see page 56)
Duxelles (see page 36)

I Preheat the oven to 400°F, 200°C, Gas Mark 6.

2 Cut the stems out of the mushrooms. (Don't throw them away: chop them and sautée in stock, sherry and soy sauce, see page 5, or use in Duxelles or Mushroom Ragout, see pages 36 and 167.) With a teaspoon, hollow out the mushrooms slightly so that they will hold a stuffing nicely. Season them lightly with salt and pepper.

3 If you are using Lentil Bolognese Sauce, Spicy Bean Dip or Duxelles, stir in 1–2 tablespoons grated Parmesan if you wish. Fill each mushroom with your chosen filling, mounding it nicely. If you wish, sprinkle a bit more Parmesan on top.

4 Tear off a piece of baking parchment that will generously enfold two of the stuffed mushrooms. Fold the paper in half and crease it along the fold. Open and mist the paper lightly and evenly with oil and water

spray. Place two mushrooms, evenly spaced, stuffing-side up, on one half of the parchment. Fold over the other half, and seal securely by folding over and crimping the edges all round, resulting in a roughly semi-circular parcel. The parcel should be roomy, but well sealed. Repeat for the remaining mushrooms. Slide the parcels on to a baking sheet, take to the oven and slide off the sheet, directly on to the oven shelf. Bake for 25–35 minutes. The parcels will darken and puff up, and the aroma will be quite wonderful.

5 When done, slide the parcels back on to the baking sheet and take to the table. With scissors, cut a cross in the top of each packet. Carefully, with a broad spatula, lift the mushrooms on to a platter. Serve at once.

(V) Omit the optional Parmesan cheese.

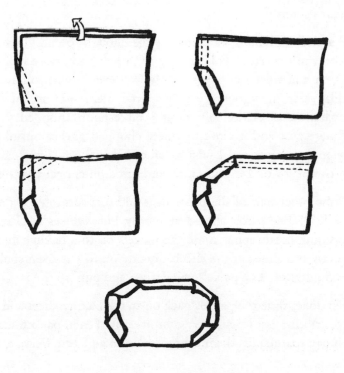

Steam-Roasted Unstuffed Mushrooms

· · · · · · · · · · · **(V)** · **(Z)** · · · · · · · · · ·

Large flat mushrooms
olive oil and water spray (see
  page 5)
chopped fresh parsley
grated orange zest
finely chopped fresh garlic

dry sherry
fresh orange juice
soy sauce or Teriyaki sauce
freshly ground black pepper

1 Preheat the oven to 400°F, 200°C, Gas Mark 6.

2 Cut the stems out of the mushrooms. (Don't throw them away: use them as suggested on page 126). With a teaspoon, hollow out the mushrooms slightly.

3 Tear a piece of baking parchment large enough to enfold two of the mushrooms in one layer. Fold the paper in half and crease it along the fold. Open and mist the paper lightly and evenly with oil and water spray. Place two mushrooms, evenly spaced, stem-side up, on one half of the parchment. Scatter on about 1 tablespoon chopped parsley, a little orange zest and 1 clove of finely chopped garlic. Sprinkle on 1 tablespoon dry sherry and 1 tablespoon orange juice, shake on a modest dash or two of soy or Teriyaki sauce, and grind on pepper to taste.

4 Fold the other half of the paper over and seal securely (as described on page 127). The parcel should be roomy, but well sealed. Repeat for the remaining mushrooms. Slide the parcels on to a baking sheet, take to the oven and slide off the sheet, directly on to the oven shelf. Bake for 25–35 minutes. The parcels will darken and puff up.

5 When done, slide the parcels back on to the baking sheet and take to the table. With scissors, cut a cross in the top of each packet. Carefully, with a broad spatula, lift the mushrooms on to a platter. Serve at once.

Grilled Vegetables

Grilling is an excellent treatment for aubergines, courgettes and peppers. They have a supple meatiness when grilled, and are useful in all sorts of sustaining main dishes. As with many of the basic ingredients in this book, it makes sense to prepare a batch of grilled vegetables once a week and to store them in the refrigerator, so they are ready for quick meals when you want them.

Grilled Aubergine

· · · · · · · · · · · · · **Ⓥ** · **Ⓩ** · · · · · · · · · · · ·

The usual method for preparing aubergine is to slice, salt to disgorge any bitterness, dry and then pan-fry the slices in a generous amount of olive oil. The aubergine soaks up the oil like a sponge so that – even though the aubergine itself has minimal calories and no fat – the oil-soaked slices add hundreds of fat calories to a dish. Grilling is an alternative, and – with the aubergines available these days – there is no bitterness, therefore no need to salt the slices first.

I aubergine, cut across into $^1/_4$ inch (5 mm) slices

olive oil and water spray (see page 5)

I Preheat the grill to the highest setting. Lightly mist a non-stick baking sheet with olive oil spray.

2 Spread out the aubergine slices in one layer on the baking sheet. *Lightly* spray the slices. Grill, close to the heat, for about 5 minutes or until they are tender and speckled with brown. Turn, mist *very* lightly with oil spray and grill for a moment or so on the second side.

Grilled Courgettes

Courgettes can be sliced and grilled in exactly the same way as aubergine.

olive oil and water spray
  (see page 5)

about 5 medium courgettes, cut
  on the slant into 1/4 inch
  (5 mm) slices

1 Preheat the grill to the highest setting. Lightly mist a non-stick baking sheet with olive oil and water spray.

2 Spread the courgette slices in one layer on the baking sheet. *Lightly* mist the slices with the spray. Grill, close to the heat, for 3–5 minutes or until the slices are tender and speckled with brown. Turn, mist *lightly* with spray, and grill for a moment or two on the second side.

Smoky Ratatouille

With a cache of mixed grilled vegetables in the fridge, you will be able to make a panful of rich, smoky ratatouille. Cut grilled aubergine slices and grilled courgette slices in half, and cut grilled peppers into strips. Stir them all into Tomato Sauce (see pages 91–2) in a saucepan. Add a handful of chopped fresh herbs, and simmer for 10–15 minutes. If you wish, spread the ratatouille in a rice crust (see page 56), top with some shreds of half-fat mozzarella, and flash under the grill to melt the cheese.

Grilled Peppers

Makes 6 halves

When grilling peppers, the point is to char *them – either directly over the gas hob, or under the grill. The burnt, blistered skin will turn quite black. When the burnt skin is slipped off, the pepper flesh below is tender and supple, smoky and sweet, and an exhilarating red (or yellow). Keep the grilled peppers covered on a plate in the fridge: they will render delicious juices that should never be wasted. Red and yellow peppers give the sweetest results. Grilled green peppers are good too, but they have a slightly bitter 'herbal' flavour.*

1 If you have a gas cooker, grill the peppers by placing them directly on the flame of the gas ring. As the peppers blacken and char, turn them with tongs. Alternatively, cut them in half, 'break' them slightly (by bending) so they lie flat, and place under the (Gas or electric) grill, cut-sides down. Grill until they blacken and char. I do mean *blackened* and *charred*. They will look awful but that is exactly how they should look. As the owner of the Carnegie Deli in New York told me years ago, '*Burning* is the secret to this kind of cooking!'

2 When blackened and charred, put the hot peppers in a plastic food bag, fold over to close the bag and leave for at least 5–10 minutes. (They can stay in the bags much longer if necessary.) Steam will form between the charred skin and the flesh, making peeling much easier. Strip off the charred skin and discard it. (Don't rinse them in water – you will only wash away the lovely smoky flavour.) Discard the cores, seeds and stems. Save any of the juices that have accumulated in the plastic bags, to use with the peppers.

DESERT ISLAND SANDWICH

I was once asked to describe my Desert Island Dish, and I didn't hesitate for even a moment. It is a sandwich. Imagine this: Roast a garlic bulb until it turns creamy and mellow (see page 136), and spread it on a crusty slice of rustic bread. Add some grilled aubergine slices, and strips of grilled red pepper, and drizzle with the pepper juices. Top with a few slices of juicy, flavourful *ripe* tomato. Cover with more beautifully crusty bread and press down. Take a big bite. Crumbs on bare bosom (this is a desert island after all!), juices down chin, sunlight and sea all around, no one to object to the after-effects of all that garlic . . . When do I leave?

QUICK PIZZA

If you can find Kool French Experience Baguette Dough (in tubes in the chill cabinet in the supermarket), make grilled vegetable pizza in minutes:

1 Preheat the oven to 400°F, 200°C, Gas Mark 6.

2 Open the tube according to the package directions, and unroll the dough. Separate into four pieces, and place them, well spaced, on a non-stick baking sheet. Spread a little tomato sauce on each, top with strips of grilled aubergine, pepper and courgette, sprinkle with half-fat mozzarella, grind on some pepper, and bake in the oven for 10–15 minutes. Garnish with basil leaves and eat with gusto!

Grilled Vegetable Mosaic

· · · · · · · · · · · · · · **V** · · · · · · · · · · · ·

Top an arrangement of grilled vegetables with an infusion of olives, garlic, balsamic vinegar and wine for a colourful main dish. Serve plenty of crusty bread to mop up the juices.

grilled red or yellow pepper halves (see page 131)

grilled courgette slices (see page 130)

grilled aubergine slices (see page 129)

10 spring onions, thinly sliced

3 black olives in brine, drained and flesh slivered off the stones

pinch of crushed dried chillies

1/2 tablespoon balsamic vinegar

2–4 garlic cloves, crushed

2 tablespoons dry red wine or dry white vermouth

1 pint (600 ml) stock

chopped fresh parsley

shredded fresh basil or mint

1 Arrange the grilled pepper halves, courgette slices and aubergine slices on an attractive platter. Take your time, and make the platter of arranged vegetables look like a stunning mosaic. Drizzle on any accumulated pepper juices.

2 Put all the remaining ingredients, except the herbs, in a heavy-bottomed frying pan. Cover and bring to the boil, then reduce the heat, and simmer for 7–10 minutes. Uncover and simmer briskly until the onions are tender and the liquid is reduced and syrupy. Pour and scrape the mixture over the grilled vegetables. Scatter the herbs over the platter.

Cheese-and-Crumb-Grilled Aubergines and Courgettes

· · · · · · · · · · · ⓥ · · · · · · · · · ·

Serves 2–3

I was visiting friends at Lake Winnipesaukee (wonderful name, wonderful place), New Hampshire, one summer (almost 30 years ago) when everyone was talking about a new way to grill fish: dip the fillets in a jar of mayonnaise, then dredge in crumbs, and grill. The mayo keeps the fish moist and succulent. Adapted to a very low-fat mayonnaise-type dressing (available in most supermarkets) and lengthways slices of aubergine and courgettes, the technique produces a show-stopping dish. The coating becomes crisp and delicious, and the texture of the vegetables – especially the aubergine – is quite wonderful. Why not try an up-market vegetarian 'fish and chip' supper with these grilled vegetables standing in for the fish, Spicy Oven-Fried Potatoes (see page 175) for the chips, Green Pea Dip (see page 37) for the mushy peas, and a bit of lemon juice or balsamic vinegar for the malt vinegar? What fun!

NOTE

If you cannot find very low-fat mayonnaise dressing, make your own. Whisk together 1 tablespoon French dark mustard with 1 tablespoon balsamic vinegar. Whisk in 16 oz (500 g) carton fat-free fromage frais and store in the fridge until needed. (If the fromage frais is fresh, it will keep for 5–6 days).

97 per cent fat-free mayonnaise

10–12 tablespoons breadcrumbs

4–5 tablespoons grated Parmesan cheese

salt and freshly ground pepper

1 long aubergine, about 8 oz (225 g)

1 long courgette, about 5 oz (150 g)

olive oil and water spray (see page 5)

lemon wedges or balsamic vinegar, to serve (optional)

1 Preheat the grill to its highest setting.

2 Spread some mayonnaise on a large plate. Put the breadcrumbs and 1–2 tablespoons of cheese on a second large plate. Season with salt and pepper (you won't need much salt; both the cheese and the mayonnaise contain plenty), and mix well.

3 Trim the ends off the aubergine and courgette. Peel them both. Cut the aubergine and courgette *lengthways* into slices about ¼ inch (5 mm) thick.

4 Lightly mist two non-stick baking sheets with the olive oil spray.

5 Dip each vegetable slice in the mayonnaise (using a rubber spatula to spread mayonnaise evenly on each side), then in the crumb and cheese mixture. Make sure both sides are well coated. Add more mayonnaise, crumbs and cheese to the plates, as needed. As the vegetable slices are done, place them on baking sheets. When they are all on the sheets, *lightly* mist the slices with olive oil spray. Position one of the baking sheets 5 inches (12.5 cm) from the grill and cook for 3–5 minutes on each side until nicely speckled with brown. (When the first side is speckled with brown, *carefully* ease a palette knife or spatula under each slice and flip it over. If part of the breadcrumbing on the underside is disturbed, sprinkle a little more crumb and cheese mixture on before sliding the baking sheet back under the grill.) Repeat with the second baking sheet.

Serve hot or cold, with lemon wedges or balsamic vinegar, if desired.

VARIATION

Courgette and Aubergine Parmesan

1 Grill the aubergine and courgette slices as above. Leave them on the baking sheets.

2 Gently spread some tomato sauce (see pages 91–2) on each slice, then top with some shredded half-fat mozzarella and a little grated Parmesan. Sprinkle with a pinch of crumbled dried oregano and grind on some pepper. Flash under the grill, to melt the cheese.

Foil-Roasted Vegetables

Roasting in foil (or, for mild onions, on a nest of foil) is another useful technique, this time for roots and bulbs. Foil-roasted garlic, in particular, is a revelation: who would guess that vulgar, rambunctious *garlic* could turn into a mellow, sweet pussycat of a vegetable?

Baked Garlic

· · · · · · · · · · · · · · · · (V) · · · · · · · · · · · · · ·

Garlic, baked whole, becomes mild and unobjectionable, and the cloves soften into a kind of purée. For this technique, buy only large, firm heads of garlic, with no sprouts and no withered cloves. Store the garlic in a ventilated basket or pierced crock in a cool part of the kitchen. (Don't refrigerate, or the bulbs will begin to sprout. And don't hold on to the garlic for months, waiting until you gather enough courage to do the deed. Baked ancient garlic is revolting.) Baked fresh, firm heads of garlic are pure pleasure. Stir the resulting purée into quark, fromage frais or yoghurt, or whirl in the processor with silken tofu to make a garlic dip or dressing. Alternatively, use it to season sauces and enrich stews and casseroles, to mash into potatoes, or to spread on bread.

large heads of firm, unblemished,
   unsprouting garlic

1 Preheat the oven to 375°F, 190°C, Gas Mark 5.

2 Remove the papery outer covering of the whole garlic heads, but do not separate the cloves or peel them. Place each whole head of garlic on a square of foil (shiny side of the foil facing in). Fold up the foil and crimp so that the garlic is wrapped in a roomy, tightly sealed pouch.

3 Bake in the oven for about 1 hour (timing depends on your oven and the size of the garlic bulb).

4 Remove from the oven, unwrap and cool for at least 5 minutes. Gently separate the cloves and squeeze each one over a fine-mesh sieve so that the softened garlic pops into the sieve.

5 With a wooden spoon or spatula, rub the garlic through the sieve into a small container or bowl. If you are in a hurry, forget the sieve, simply squeeze the garlic into the bowl, and push it into a mound with a rubber spatula. Cover tightly with cling film and refrigerate until the purée is needed.

GARLIC IS GOOD FOR YOU

Not only is garlic a culinary gem, but it is also believed to have significant health benefits. There are many studies in medical literature implicating garlic as an agent in cholesterol and blood pressure control, and as an antibacterial, antifungal, and possibly anticarcinogenic agent. Judging from the majority of evidence, it's natural garlic – smell and all – that has therapeutic properties.

Baked Onion

· · · · · · · · · · · · · ○ · · · · · · · · · · · · ·

There are few things sweeter than a baked onion. Eat it cut into quarters and sprinkled with balsamic vinegar, or purée it in a blender and stir into mashed potatoes or puréed root vegetable gratins.

large mild, Spanish-type onions
freshly ground pepper and lemon
  juice, to serve

1 Preheat the oven to 400°F, 200°C, Gas Mark 6.

2 Put the onions on a double sheet of foil, shiny side out, on a baking sheet, but do not wrap them. Bake in the oven for 1¼ hours or until very soft and almost collapsed.

3 With a sharp knife, cut off the stem and root ends of the onions. Remove and discard the blackened skin and first layer of each one. Serve the onions as they are, with pepper and lemon juice, or put them in a blender, and purée for use in other recipes.

Clockwise from top Cauliflower and Peppers (page 152), Bread and Caramelised Onion Pudding (page 88), Italian Sweet and Sour Courgettes (page 149)

Opposite page 139, clockwise from top Sweet Rice Pulao (page 60), Fruit and Fennel Chutney (page 190), Vegetable Curry with Corn Cobs (page 162), Mint and Coriander Riata (page 191), Green Split Pea Dhal (page 113)

Baked Beetroot

· · · · · · · · · · · · V · · · · · · · · · · · · ·

Beetroots are a dark, earthy red, with a deep earthy taste – at their best purchased raw, wrapped in foil and baked. Baked beetroot makes a wonderful dip or spread: cut it into chunks and place in a blender or food processor with a spoonful or two of fromage frais or yoghurt, a splash of lemon juice or good wine vinegar, and a bit of raw garlic (or baked garlic purée, see page 136), if you wish. Season with salt and pepper, and process to a rough, chunky purée. Add more fromage frais, lemon juice or wine vinegar and seasonings, as needed. The colour, texture and taste make this a knock-out. Baked beetroot is excellent, as well, sliced and dressed with a mixture of balsamic vinegar, lime and orange juice, or with fromage frais mixed with chopped fresh herbs.

medium-sized raw beetroots

1 Preheat the oven to 400°F, 200°C, Gas Mark 6.

2 Trim the beetroot greens away, scrub and wrap the whole, unpeeled beetroots in foil, shiny side in (3–4 beetroots may go in one package).

3 Bake in the oven for 1–2 hours or until tender. (Timing depends on the age and size of the beetroots.) Use a skewer to test if the beetroots are done. The skewer should go in easily but the beetroots should not be mushy. Leave to cool, then trim and slip off the skins.

Foil-Roasted Root Vegetables

· · · · · · · · · · · · · · · ⓥ · · · · · · · · · · · · · · ·

Roasting root vegetables in this manner brings out their natural sweetness and flavour as does no other method. This technique works for swedes, turnips, celeriac, carrots and parsnips. The baked vegetables may be served as they are, or mashed and whipped with buttermilk or fromage frais, or mashed with an equal amount of potatoes. If you love garlic, beat in some baked garlic purée (see page 136) as well.

Foil-roasted roots have a gloriously intense and deep taste. My advice is to bake batches of the foil-roasted roots every once in a while, and to keep them in the refrigerator to use during the week. It makes as much good sense as keeping cooked rice, canned beans and frozen tomato sauce on hand. With a little pre-planning, sustaining, nutritious, comforting meals are so much easier to throw together at the end of a busy day.

root vegetables: swedes, turnips,
  celeriac, carrots or parsnips

1 Preheat the oven to 425°F, 220°C, Gas Mark 7.

2 Peel the root vegetables you have chosen. Small roots such as turnips, carrots and small parsnips may be left whole; large ones, such as large parsnips, swedes and celeriac, should be cut into quarters. Wrap two or three single vegetables or two vegetable quarters loosely in foil, shiny-side in. Crimp well, so that you have a tightly sealed but roomy pouch. Repeat for the remaining vegetables. Bake in the oven for 1–1¼ hours or until the vegetables are very tender and beginning to caramelise around the edges.

Gratins of Foil-Roasted Roots

Purées of foil-roasted roots can be put together in all sorts of ways, with all sorts of seasonings, to make warming gratins. Several examples follow. They are hard to improve upon at the centre of a meal, flanked by contrasting accompaniments. Mushroom Ragout (see page 167) and Stir-Fried Peppers (see page 151) go especially well with these gratins.

Simple Gratin of Foil-Roasted Vegetables

. . . . Z . . . .

Serves 4

5 foil-roasted white turnips (see page 140)

6 foil-roasted medium carrots (see page 140)

purée from one head of roasted garlic (see page 136)

2–3 tablespoons buttermilk or fromage frais

salt and freshly ground pepper

4 tablespoons grated Parmesan cheese

1 Preheat the oven to 350°F, 180°C, Gas Mark 4 (unless preparing ahead of time, see step 3).

2 Purée the vegetables in a blender or food processor until smooth. Add the buttermilk or fromage frais and purée again until well blended. Season with salt and pepper.

3 Scrape the mixture into a small gratin dish or shallow baking dish. Smooth the top and sprinkle with the Parmesan. (The dish may be prepared ahead of time to this point. Refrigerate, well covered, until needed. It will keep for up to two days. Bring to room temperature before proceeding.)

4 Bake, uncovered, in the oven for 30–45 minutes or until browned on top and thoroughly hot. (If you wish, to save time, the gratin can be heated in the microwave, then browned under a hot grill.)

Gratin of Baked Potatoes, Onions and Garlic

. . . .

Serves 4

My favourite gratin combines baked potatoes, onions and garlic. Sweetly earthy, it glorifies mashed potatoes.

4 baking potatoes, baked and mashed (see page 173)

purée from 1 head of roasted garlic (see page 136)

2 mild onions, baked and puréed (see page 138)

4 tablespoons grated Parmesan cheese

salt and freshly ground pepper

2–3 tablespoons buttermilk or fromage frais

skimmed milk

1 Preheat the oven to 350°F, 180°C, Gas Mark 4 (unless preparing ahead of time, see step 3).

2 Put the potato, garlic, onion and cheese in a bowl. Season with salt and pepper, and beat with a wooden spoon. Beat in the buttermilk or fromage frais.

3 Scrape the mixture into a gratin dish and smooth the surface. (The recipe may be prepared in advance to this stage and refrigerated, covered, until needed. Bring to room temperature before proceeding.) Dribble a little skimmed milk evenly over the top of the vegetables. Bake, uncovered, in the oven for 30–40 minutes or until brown, bubbly and thoroughly hot. (If you wish, to save time, heat through in the microwave, then brown under a hot grill.)

Curried Gratin of Foil-Roasted Vegetables

· · · · · · · · · · · · · ❷ · · · · · · · · · · · · ·

Serves 4

A curry infusion (below), or an infusion of Italian seasonings (following recipe), changes the character of roasted vegetable gratins. As you learn the versatility of this technique, you will be able to improvise many different versions.

1 onion, chopped

1/2 teaspoon each of ground coriander, ground cumin, mild chilli powder, paprika and ground ginger

salt and freshly ground pepper

1/4 teaspoon ground turmeric

1/4 teaspoon ground allspice

pinch of cayenne pepper (or to taste)

1/2 pint (300 ml) stock

2 foil-roasted small white turnips, puréed or mashed (see page 140)

purée from 1 head of foil-roasted garlic (see page 136)

2 foil-roasted carrots, puréed or mashed (see page 140)

3 foil-roasted small parsnips, puréed or mashed (see page 140)

1/2 foil-roasted small swede, puréed or mashed (see page 140)

2–3 tablespoons buttermilk or fromage frais

2–3 tablespoons skimmed milk

1 Preheat the oven to 400°F, 200°C, Gas Mark 6.

2 Put the onion, spices and stock in a heavy-bottomed frying pan. Cover, bring to boil, and boil for 5–7 minutes. Uncover, reduce heat, and simmer until the onions are tender and the liquid almost gone.

3 Combine the onion and spice mixture with all the puréed vegetables. (To purée the vegetables, cut them into chunks and purée in a blender or food processor until very smooth. Alternatively, mash with a potato masher.) Beat in the buttermilk or fromage frais, then spread the mixture in a gratin dish.

4 Pour a thin drizzle of milk evenly over the top and bake for 30–45 minutes or until bubbly, puffy and browned. (If you wish, to save time, heat through in the microwave, and brown under a hot grill.)

Italian Root Vegetable Gratin

· · · · · · · · · · · · · · ⓩ · · · · · · · · · · · · · ·

Serves 4

The tried and tested sun-dried tomato–spring onion infusion is used without garlic in this gratin, because roasted garlic purée is added to the vegetable mixture. Swedes and turnips are not particularly Italian, but the infusion bestows upon them an honorary Italian aura.

2–3 dry-packed sun-dried tomatoes, coarsely chopped (use scissors)

pinch of crushed dried chillies

pinch of dried oregano

6 spring onions, sliced

$1/2$ pint (300 ml) stock

6 foil-roasted carrots (see page 140)

3 foil-roasted small white turnips (see page 140)

$1/2$ foil-roasted small swede (see page 140)

purée from 1 head of foil-roasted garlic (see page 136)

3 tablespoons fromage frais

salt and freshly ground pepper

2 tablespoons grated Parmesan cheese

a few tablespoons of skimmed milk

1 Preheat the oven to 425°F, 220°C, Gas Mark 7.

2 Put the sun-dried tomatoes, chilli, oregano, spring onions and stock in a heavy-bottomed frying pan. Cover, bring to the boil, and boil for 5–7 minutes. Uncover, reduce the heat, and simmer until the onion is tender, and the liquid almost gone. Leave to cool slightly.

3 Put this infusion in a food processor or blender with the foil-roasted vegetables, garlic and fromage frais, and process to a purée. Season with salt and pepper.

4 Spread the mixture in a gratin dish. Sprinkle with Parmesan cheese and pour a thin drizzle of milk evenly over the top of the gratin.

5 Bake in the oven for 30–45 minutes or until bubbly, puffy and browned on top. (To save time, heat through in the microwave, and then brown under a hot grill.)

Oven-Braised Vegetables

Oven-braising in stock in an open baking dish is another fat-free method of making the most of various vegetables' natural goodness. Three examples follow, but you could also apply the method to thickly sliced (or quartered) courgettes; peeled and quartered kohlrabi; and cauliflower florets.

Oven-Braised Fennel

. . . .

Serves 4

Fennel looks like bulbous celery and tastes of anise. There is a scene in the film Star Wars, *when Luke Skywalker is at home on Tatooine, and his Aunt Beru prepares a meal by putting bulbs of fennel into a sort of other-worldly food processor. I suppose director George Lucas thought that a vegetable resembling alien celery was just right for extra-terrestrial home cooking!*

2 fennel bulbs, cut in half lengthways
4 fl oz (100 ml) stock

salt and freshly ground pepper
3 tablespoons grated Parmesan cheese

1 Preheat the oven to 350°F, 180°C, Gas Mark 4.

2 Cut each fennel half into wedges about ¹/₂ inch (1 cm) wide. Arrange the fennel in one layer in a baking dish. Pour over the stock and season with salt and pepper.

3 Bake, uncovered, in the oven for 45 minutes, sprinkling the Parmesan over the fennel for the last 15 minutes. The fennel will become meltingly tender and the stock will have cooked almost completely away, leaving a rich glaze. Serve at once.

✔ Omit the Parmesan cheese.

Oven-Braised Aubergine, Chinese-Style

Ⓥ

Makes 2 pints (1.1 litres) Serves 4

Aubergine's sponge-like character is perfect for oven-braising – it soaks up the Chinese flavourings most deliciously.

6 small aubergines, cut into 1 inch (2.5 cm) cubes

3 garlic cloves, crushed

½ inch (1 cm) piece of fresh root ginger, peeled and crushed

1 tablespoon Teriyaki sauce

3 tablespoons medium dry sherry

8 fl oz (225 ml) stock

freshly ground pepper

1 Preheat the oven to 350°F, 180°C, Gas Mark 4.

2 Spread the aubergine in a shallow baking or gratin dish. Mix the remaining ingredients together and pour over the aubergine. Bake, uncovered, in the oven for 45 minutes–1 hour or until the aubergine is tender and deeply delicious, shaking the pan and stirring up the vegetable pieces occasionally. Serve hot.

Oven-Braised Jerusalem Artichokes

· · · · · · · · · · · · **V** · · · · · · · · · · ·

Jerusalem Artichokes are rough, knobbly roots that are neither artichokes, nor from Jerusalem, although their flavour does bear some resemblance to that of French globe artichokes. Their texture is pleasurably starchy, although one of the starches they contain is inulin, which makes some people very 'windy' – others don't seem bothered at all. You don't know until you try them – and they really are very good to eat.

olive oil and water spray (see page 5)
stock

Jerusalem artichokes, peeled and halved
freshly ground pepper (optional)

I Preheat the oven to 200°C, 400°F, Gas Mark 6.

2 Mist a baking dish with olive oil spray, and pour in a few tablespoons of stock. Put the artichokes in, cut-sides down, and roast in the oven for 35–45 minutes or until they are tender, browned and sizzling, stirring occasionally. If necessary, add a few more drops of stock now and then, but don't swamp the artichokes.

3 Season with pepper, if desired, and serve.

Stir-Frying in Stock

Stir-frying usually depends on oil, but it can easily be done with stock, either in a wok or in a large frying pan. Some vegetables (courgettes and peppers, for example) can just be tossed around in stock (and whatever seasoning you like) until they are tender and the liquid has cooked down. Others (cauliflower and broccoli, for example) need a combination of stir-frying and simmering to reach tenderness. It is an option to steam the vegetable to partial tenderness first, and then quickly to stir-fry in a flavourful infusion to finish it off. Several recipes follow, to get you started.

Stir-Fried Courgettes

· · · · · · · · · · · · · · · **(V)** · · **(Z)** · · · · · · · · · · · · · · ·

Serves 2–4

6 small courgettes
4 fl oz (100 ml) stock
salt and freshly ground pepper

generous pinch of ground cumin
juice of 1 lime

1 Wash and trim the courgettes but do not peel them. Cut them in half and then into strips about 2 inches (5 cm) long and ½ inch (1 cm) wide.

2 Pour the stock into a heavy-bottomed frying pan or wok, and bring to the boil. Throw in the courgettes, grind in a generous amount of pepper, and sprinkle in the cumin. With two wooden spoons, constantly toss and turn the vegetables over high heat until they are crisp–tender, and the stock has cooked down to almost nothing. Squeeze in the lime juice, season lightly with salt and let the courgettes stir-'fry' for a minute or so in their own juices.

Stir-Fried Courgettes with Garlic and Ginger

Crush a clove of garlic and a thin slice of peeled root ginger. Put them in a frying pan with the stock and 1 fl oz (25 ml) dry sherry, and boil for a few seconds before throwing in the courgettes. Omit the pepper and the lime juice. Sprinkle with some chopped fresh coriander before serving.

Italian Sweet and Sour Courgettes

Add two cloves of crushed garlic to the stock and boil for a few seconds. Throw in the courgettes, freshly ground pepper, 2 tablespoons each of sultanas, capers (drained and rinsed), and the juice of 1 lemon. Just before serving, stir in some finely chopped parsley. Serve hot or cold.

Stir-Fried Cauliflower

V · Z

Serves 2 – 4

In this stir-fry, cauliflower is given the full no-fat Italian treatment. Because cauliflower is such a good flavour absorber, it takes deliciously to this treatment.

½ pint (300 ml) stock

4 spring onions, sliced

pinch of crushed dried chillies (optional)

1 garlic clove, crushed

2 black olives in brine, drained and flesh slivered off the stones

2 dry-packed sun-dried tomatoes, chopped (use scissors)

1 large cauliflower, separated into florets

salt and freshly ground pepper

1 Put 6 fl oz (175 ml) of the stock, the spring onions, chilli, garlic, olive pieces and sun-dried tomatoes in a wide heavy-bottomed frying pan or wok. Bring to the boil and boil for 4–5 minutes. Toss in the cauliflower, and season with salt and pepper. Add the remaining stock, cover and simmer for 3 minutes.

2 Uncover the pan and turn the heat to high. Stir and toss the florets in the boiling stock until the stock is almost gone and the cauliflower is crisp–tender.

Stir-Fried Peppers

· · · · · · · · · · · · · **V** · · **Z** · · · · · · · · · · · · · ·

Makes ³/₄ pint (450 ml)

Peppers take to stock stir-frying remarkably well. The juices cook down to a buttery sauce-like consistency and the pepper pieces become supple and lusciously tender. Stir-fried peppers make an excellent side dish, as well as a colourful garnish for many other dishes. The technique only works if the peppers have been peeled.

4–6 red or yellow peppers
6–8 fl oz (175–225 ml) stock

freshly ground pepper

1 Cut the peppers lengthways in half. Remove the stems, the seeds and the ribs, and cut the halves into their natural sections. Peel each piece with a swivel-bladed vegetable peeler, then cut into strips about ¹/₂ inch (1 cm) wide.

2 Heat the stock in a heavy-bottomed frying pan. When very hot, toss in the peppers and grind in some black pepper. Stir and turn the peppers in the hot stock until the liquid has cooked down considerably. Turn down the heat a little and 'fry' the peppers in their own juices for a few minutes or until they are very tender, and the pepper juices have formed a thick sauce. Serve at once, with their delicious juices, or serve at room temperature. This dish may be made in advance and rewarmed later or on the next day.

Cauliflower and Peppers

Serves 4

Cauliflower and peppers make a stunning pair. For a change, substitute fennel or anise seeds for the cumin.

1 large cauliflower, separated into florets

2 large red peppers, deseeded and cut lengthways into their natural sections

6 fl oz (175 ml) stock

1 garlic clove, crushed

1/2 teaspoon cumin seeds

salt and freshly ground pepper

1 Steam the cauliflower florets over boiling water for about 5 minutes or until partially cooked. Refresh under cold running water and set aside.

2 With a swivel-bladed vegetable peeler, peel each pepper piece. Cut the peppers into strips about 1/2 inch (1 cm) wide.

3 Heat half the stock in a heavy-bottomed frying pan. When it begins to bubble, stir in the garlic and peppers. Stir and toss with two wooden spoons until the peppers are almost tender and the liquid almost gone. Lower the heat and leave the peppers to 'fry' gently in their own juices as you stir them. When they are tender, stir in the cauliflower.

4 Sprinkle in the cumin and stir well. Pour in the remaining stock, stir and cook until the cauliflower is tender but not mushy. Season with salt and pepper.

Peperonata

· · · · · · · · · · · · · · · **V** · · **Z** · · · · · · · · · · · ·

Makes 1¹/₄ pints (750 ml)/ Serves 4

The addition of onion, vermouth, olives and capers turns stir-fried peppers into a vibrant Italian side dish.

6 large red peppers
1 large mild onion
2 garlic cloves, crushed
2 black olives in brine, drained and flesh slivered off the stones
2 fl oz (50 ml) dry white vermouth

6 fl oz (175 ml) stock
1 tablespoon drained capers
salt and freshly ground pepper
2 tablespoons chopped fresh parsley

1 Cut the peppers lengthways in half. Remove the stems, the seeds and the ribs, and cut the halves into their natural sections. Peel with a swivel-bladed vegetable peeler, and cut each piece into strips about ¹/₂ inch (1 cm) wide. Cut the onion in half, and then cut each half into thin half-moons.

2 Put the peppers, onion, garlic, olives, vermouth, stock and capers in a heavy-bottomed frying pan. Grind in some pepper and bring to the boil, then reduce the heat and cook the vegetables, tossing and turning them in the stock until the liquid has cooked down considerably.

3 Let the vegetables 'fry' in their own juices until beautifully tender. Salt lightly, if necessary, and stir in the parsley. Serve hot or cold as a salad, a relish, a sandwich filling or a vegetable.

Stir-Fried Asparagus

. . . . V . . . .

*The best way to treat asparagus is to prepare the stalks as in step 1,
below, then to steam them over boiling water for 3–7 minutes only
(depending on their size) until they just bend a little when lifted with
tongs. Blot dry with absorbent kitchen paper, and serve with Yellow
Pepper Sauce (see page 100). Pick up each stalk with your fingers,
dabble in the sauce, and eat. The stir-frying method described below is
the next best method. During the asparagus season, alternate the
methods (or have one for lunch, one for dinner, if you are as much of an
asparagus fanatic as I am).*

fresh, thick asparagus
3–4 fl oz (75–100 ml) stock
¹/₂ lime

pinch of dried thyme
pinch of dried tarragon
salt and freshly ground pepper

1 Cut off the tough, woody, bottom portion of each asparagus stalk.
With a swivel-bladed vegetable peeler, peel each stalk from the bottom
up to the tip. If you are not going to cook the stalks at once, stand them
in a glass of water as if they were a bunch of flowers.

2 Cut the asparagus into 1 inch (2.5 cm) lengths. Heat the stock in a
non-reactive wok or frying pan. Throw in the asparagus and toss and
turn in the hot stock for about 2 minutes (use two wooden spoons or
spatulas).

3 Squeeze in the juice of ¹/₂ lime, add a pinch each of thyme and
tarragon, and season with salt and pepper. Continue to stir-fry for a few
moments more or until the asparagus is crisp–tender (more crisp than
tender). Serve at once.

Glazed Turnips

. . . . V . . . .

Makes 1 pint (600 ml)/Serves 2–4

Both turnips and carrots benefit from stir-frying in a mixture of stock, citrus juice and complementary seasonings. The turnips are boiled in this flavourful mixture first, then simmered and stirred until tender and glazed; the carrots (below) are simply stir-fried.

1½ lb (700 g) small white turnips, peeled and cut into ½ inch (1 cm) wedges
½ pint (300 ml) stock

2 fl oz (50 ml) orange juice
1 tablespoon hoisin sauce
1 teaspoon sugar
salt and freshly ground pepper

1 Put all the ingredients in a frying pan that can be covered. Cover, bring to the boil, and boil for 7–8 minutes.

2 Uncover, reduce the heat, and simmer, stirring occasionally, until the turnips are meltingly tender and bathed in a syrupy glaze.

Spiced Carrots

. . . . V . . Z . . . .

Makes 1 pint (600 ml)/Serves 2–4

1 pint (600 ml) stock
4 garlic cloves, crushed
½ teaspoon ground cumin
pinch of ground cinnamon
pinch of cayenne pepper

½ teaspoon sugar
juice of 1 small lemon
1 lb (450 g) carrots, sliced
salt and freshly ground pepper

1 Put all the ingredients except the carrots, salt and pepper, in a heavy-bottomed saucepan. Cover, bring to the boil, and boil for 3–4 minutes.

2 Uncover, stir in the carrots and season with salt and pepper. Cook, uncovered, stirring and tossing, until the carrots are tender, and the liquid has cooked down to a syrupy glaze.

Curries and Stews

Go vegetable mad! Sweep down the greengrocery aisles and gather up armfuls of the best-looking roots, bulbs, shoots, greens, reds and yellows. Bring the vegetable treasure home for peeling, dicing and slicing, then toss them into infusions of herbs and spices and cook until they soak up all the spicy flavour, yet their own vegetable goodness shines through. Serve heaped platters of these steamy, fragrant stews and curries with rice or other grains, along with a chutney or salsa or two, and fromage frais mixed with a few chopped herbs.

SERVING NOTE

Serving size depends on appetite, and how many other dishes will be served with the stew. For a main dish mixed-vegetable curry or stew, $^{3}/_{4}$–1 pint (450–600 ml) equals one serving; for a single-vegetable curry, like Curried Cabbage (below) and Mushroom Ragout (see page 167), about $^{1}/_{2}$ pint (300 ml) equals one serving because they are best served as part of a selection of vegetable dishes. These are *very* general rules.

Curried Cabbage

. . . .

Makes 1 pint (600 ml)

The important thing, when preparing fat-free curries, is to ensure that the onions and curry spices cook gently in stock long enough for the spices to lose their harsh, raw character. It only takes 10–12 minutes altogether, but they are important *minutes.*

1 large onion, halved and cut into thin half-moons

2 garlic cloves, crushed

$^{1}/_{4}$ teaspoon each mild chilli powder, ground cinnamon, ground turmeric and ground ginger

pinch of ground allspice

1 teaspoon paprika

1 teaspoon ground cumin

$^{1}/_{2}$ teaspoon ground coriander

1 pint (600 ml) stock

1 small white cabbage, cored, trimmed of tough outer leaves, quartered, and shredded (use a sharp kitchen knife, or the *slicing* blade of a food processor)

$^{1}/_{4}$–$^{1}/_{2}$ lime

salt and freshly ground pepper

1 Put the onion, garlic, spices and ½ pint (300 ml) stock in a heavy-bottomed frying pan. Cover, bring to the boil, and boil for 5–7 minutes. Reduce the heat a little and simmer, stirring frequently, until the vegetables and spices are 'frying' in their own juices.

2 Stir in the cabbage and remaining stock. Simmer, uncovered, for 15–20 minutes or until the cabbage is tender and the sauce is thick and savoury. Squeeze in a little lime juice, taste and adjust the seasonings.

Curried Cauliflower

· · · · · · · · · · · **Ⓥ** · · **Ⓩ** · · · · · · · · · · · ·

Makes 1 pint (600 ml)

Potatoes and cauliflower are able to soak up beautiful spice infusions without losing their own character. In this recipe, the cauliflower soaks alone; in the following recipe, it pairs up with its rival.

1 mild onion, chopped
3 garlic cloves, crushed
½ teaspoon ground turmeric
2 teaspoons ground coriander
1 teaspoon ground cumin
1 teaspoon garam masala
¼ teaspoon cayenne pepper

½ pint (300 ml) stock
14 oz (400 g) can of chopped tomatoes
1 large cauliflower, separated into florets
salt and freshly ground pepper

1 Put the onion, garlic, spices and stock in a heavy-bottomed frying pan. Cover, bring to the boil, and boil for 5–7 minutes. Uncover, reduce the heat a little, and simmer, stirring frequently, until the onions and spices are 'frying' in their own juices.

2 Stir in the tomatoes and the cauliflower, and season with salt and pepper. Cover and simmer for 15 minutes. Uncover and simmer, stirring occasionally, for an additional 15–20 minutes or until the cauliflower is tender and the sauce thick and savoury.

Potato and Cauliflower Curry

· · · · · · · · · · · · · · · **V** · · **Z** · · · · · · · · · · · · · ·

Makes 3 pints (1.7 litres)

Serve this with the usual: rice, raita, a chutney (or two or three), and finish with something indulgently fruity – a mango, or a handful of fresh lychees.

3 large onions, each cut into 8 wedges

$\frac{1}{2}$ inch (1 cm) piece of fresh root ginger, peeled and crushed

2 garlic cloves, crushed

$\frac{1}{2}$ teaspoon ground turmeric

$\frac{1}{4}$ teaspoon cayenne pepper

$1\frac{1}{2}$ teaspoons ground coriander

$\frac{1}{2}$ teaspoon ground cardamom

$\frac{1}{2}$ teaspoon ground allspice

1 pint (600 ml) stock

1 tablespoon tomato purée

1 medium cauliflower, separated into florets

3 medium all-purpose (e.g. Wilja) potatoes, scrubbed and cut into $\frac{1}{2}$ inch (1 cm) cubes

salt and freshly ground pepper

chopped fresh coriander, to garnish

1 Put the onions, ginger, garlic, spices and $\frac{1}{2}$ pint (300 ml) stock in a heavy-bottomed frying pan. Cover, bring to the boil, and boil for 5–7 minutes. Uncover, reduce the heat, and simmer, stirring occasionally, until the onions and spices are 'frying' in their own juices. Stir in the tomato purée.

2 Purée half the mixture in a blender or food processor, and return it to the pan.

3 Stir in the cauliflower, potato and remaining stock. Cover and simmer, stirring occasionally, until the vegetables are tender and the sauce is thick and savoury. Season with salt and pepper, and serve garnished with coriander.

Vegetable Curry

· · · · · · · · · · ·V· ·Z· · · · · · · · · · ·

Makes 3 pints (1.7 litres)

The next three recipes, for mixed vegetable curries, take full advantage of our modern vegetable bounty, and the no-fat onion–spice sauté method. This mixture features fennel, cauliflower and courgettes.

1 large mild onion, coarsely chopped

2–4 garlic cloves, crushed

1½ teaspoons ground cumin

1½ teaspoons ground coriander

¼ teaspoon ground allspice

¼ teaspoon cayenne pepper

½ teaspoon ground ginger

1 teaspoon ground turmeric

1 teaspoon paprika

24 fl oz (700 ml) stock

3 celery stalks, cut into ½ inch (1 cm) slices

3 carrots, coarsely chopped

3 small white turnips, peeled and coarsely chopped

3 peppers (1 red, 1 green, 1 yellow) peeled, deseeded and coarsely chopped

1 fennel bulb, cut into ½ inch (1 cm) slices

1 lb (450 g) courgettes, cut into ½ inch (1 cm) slices

1 small cauliflower, separated into florets

juice of 1 medium lemon

salt and freshly ground pepper

6 tablespoons chopped fresh parsley

4 tablespoons chopped fresh coriander

1 Put the onion, garlic, spices and ½ pint (300 ml) stock in a heavy-bottomed frying pan. Cover, bring to the boil, and boil for 5–7 minutes. Stir in the celery, carrots, turnips, peppers and fennel, reduce the heat a little, and simmer, stirring frequently, until the vegetables and spices are 'frying' in their own juices.

2 Stir in the remaining ingredients, except the herbs but including the remaining 14 fl oz (400 ml) stock. Season with salt and pepper, and simmer gently, covered, for 20–25 minutes or until all the vegetables are tender. Stir in the herbs just before serving.

Vegetable Curry in Vegetable Sauce

· · · · · · · · · · · · **◉** · · · · · · · · · · · ·

Makes 4 pints (2.3 litres)

The rich sauce for this curry is produced by puréeing some of the spice-infused vegetables, very simple to do with a blender or food processor.

2 large mild onions, each cut into 8 pieces

2 garlic cloves, crushed

1 tablespoon each of ground cumin, ground coriander and paprika

1/2 teaspoon each of ground allspice, ground cardamom and ground ginger

1 teaspoon ground turmeric

1/4 teaspoon cayenne pepper (or to taste)

about 1 pint (600 ml) stock

3 medium peppers, peeled, deseeded and coarsely chopped

3 large carrots, coarsely chopped

12 oz (350 g) button mushrooms, halved or quartered

2 medium white turnips, cut into 1/2 inch (1 cm) pieces

1 large cauliflower, separated into florets

1 small parsnip, cut into 1/2 inch (1 cm) pieces

1 fennel bulb, quartered and cut into 1/2 inch (1 cm) slices

3 celery stalks, cut into 1/2 inch (1 cm) slices

salt

juice of 1/2 large lemon

3 medium courgettes, cut into 1/2 inch (1 cm) slices

8 oz (225 g) runner beans, cut into 1/2 inch (1 cm) pieces

Mint and Coriander Raita (see page 191) or Creamy Herb Sauce (see page 192), to garnish

1 Put the onion pieces, garlic, spices and 1/2 pint (300 ml) stock in a heavy-bottomed saucepan. Cover, bring to the boil, and boil for 5–7 minutes. Uncover and stir in the peppers, carrots and mushrooms. Reduce the heat slightly and simmer, stirring frequently, until the vegetables and spices are 'frying' in their own juices, and the vegetables are tender. Leave to cool slightly.

2 Purée half the mixture in a blender or food processor, then return the purée to the pan.

3 Add the turnip, cauliflower, parsnip, fennel and celery. Stir together very well. Add enough stock almost to cover the contents of the pot, season with salt, and bring to the boil.

4 Reduce the heat, cover, and simmer for 15 minutes. Uncover, squeeze in the lemon juice, and add the courgettes and beans. Simmer, uncovered for 10 minutes more, or until all the vegetables are tender. Serve in deep soup bowls, each serving garnished with a dollop of Raita or Creamy Herb Sauce.

(V) Omit the Raita or Creamy Herb Sauce

Vegetable Curry with Corn Cobs

. . . . ❼ . . . .

Makes 3¹/₂ pints (2 litres)

Adorable dwarf sweetcorn cobs (which can be eaten whole) star in this curry, along with co-stars fennel and mushrooms, and the usual carrots and celery. Parsnips and turnips make appearances, too. You could eat a vegetable curry or chilli every night for a year, and never repeat yourself, and never grow bored – at least I could!

2 mild onions, coarsely chopped

4 garlic cloves, crushed

1 teaspoon mild chilli powder

1 teaspoon dried oregano

1 tablespoon paprika

1 tablespoon ground coriander

¹/₂ teaspoon ground cinnamon

¹/₄ teaspoon ground allspice

pinch of ground cloves

2 teaspoons ground cumin

³/₄ pint (450 ml) stock

3 celery stalks, cut into ¹/₂ inch (1 cm) slices

3 carrots, coarsely chopped

1 fennel bulb, quartered and cut into ¹/₂ inch (1 cm) slices

8 oz (225 g) button mushrooms, halved or quartered

3 peppers (1 red, 1 yellow, 1 green), peeled, deseeded and coarsely chopped, or use canned peppers (pimentos)

two 14 oz (400 g) cans of chopped tomatoes

2 medium white turnips, chopped into ¹/₂ inch (1 cm) cubes

1 small parsnip, chopped into ¹/₂ inch (1 cm) cubes

salt and freshly ground pepper

8 dwarf sweetcorn cobs, sliced into 1 inch (2.5 cm) pieces

8 oz (225 g) runner beans, cut into 1 inch (2.5 cm) pieces

Mint and Coriander Raita (see page 191) and thinly sliced spring onions, to garnish

1 Put the onion pieces, garlic, spices and ¹/₂ pint (300 ml) stock in a heavy-bottomed saucepan. Cover, bring to the boil, and boil for 5–7 minutes. Uncover and stir in the celery, carrots, fennel, mushrooms, peppers and a bit more stock. Simmer, stirring occasionally, until the vegetables and spices are 'frying' in their own juices. Cook gently for a few more minutes, stirring.

2 Stir in the tomatoes, turnip and parsnip. Season with salt and pepper, and simmer for 10 minutes.

3 Stir in the corn cobs and runner beans. Simmer for about another 10 minutes or until all the vegetables are tender. Serve in soup bowls, each garnished with a dollop of Raita and a sprinkling of spring onions.

🅥 Omit the Raita

Vegetable Chilli with Potatoes

· · · · · · · · · · · ❷ · · · · · · · · · · ·

Makes 3 ¹/₂ pints (2 litres)

The so-called 'Tex-Mex' food that passes for Mexican cuisine in popular restaurants is really no indication of how good real Mexican food can be. It is a complex and interesting cuisine based on spice pastes, chillies and ground seeds and nuts – in some ways reminiscent of the cuisines of parts of India. Like Indian cuisine (indeed like most of the world's cuisines), it is fat-based, but – again like most cuisines – it adapts well to low-fat techniques.

1 mild onion, coarsely chopped

2–4 garlic cloves, crushed

3 celery stalks, cut into ¹/₂ inch (1 cm) slices

3 carrots, coarsely chopped

1 tablespoon each of paprika, mild chilli powder and ground cumin

¹/₂ tablespoon ground coriander

¹/₄ teaspoon ground cinnamon

1 teaspoon dried oregano

about ¹/₂ pint (300 ml) stock

3 peppers (1 red, 1 yellow, 1 green), peeled, deseeded and coarsely chopped

two 14 oz (400 g) cans of chopped tomatoes

2 all-purpose (e.g. Wilja) potatoes, cut into 1 inch (2.5 cm) cubes

4 small courgettes, cut into ¹/₂ inch (1 cm) slices

1 large cauliflower, separated into florets

salt and freshly ground pepper

fromage frais and chopped fresh coriander, to garnish

1 Put the onion, garlic, celery, carrots, spices, oregano and ¹/₂ pint (300 ml) stock in a heavy-bottomed frying pan. Cover, bring to the boil, and boil for 5–7 minutes. Uncover, stir in the peppers, and simmer, stirring frequently, until the vegetables and spices are 'frying' in their own juices.

2 Stir in the tomatoes and potatoes. Simmer for 5 minutes, then stir in the courgettes and cauliflower. Season with salt and pepper, and add a little more stock, if necessary. Simmer for 20–25 minutes or until the mixture is thick and the cauliflower and potatoes are tender. Serve with small bowls of the garnishes.

Ⓥ Omit the fromage frais garnish

Lesco–Potato Stew

· · · · · · · · · · · · · · · ⊘ · · · · · · · · · · · · · · ·

Makes 3 pints (1.7 litres)

Lesco is a Hungarian mélange of onions, peppers and paprika (plus lard or goose fat, but let's not dwell on that). Hungarians seem to cook lesco with everything, which is not a bad thing – it is delicious. Lesco goes particularly well with potatoes (but then, most things go particularly well with potatoes).

3 large mild onions, coarsely chopped

2 garlic cloves, crushed

2 tablespoons paprika

1 teaspoon dried marjoram

about ³/₄ pint (450 ml) stock

3 large peppers (1 red, 1 green, 1 yellow), peeled, deseeded and coarsely chopped

salt and freshly ground pepper

1–2 pinches of cayenne pepper (optional)

two 14 oz (400 g) cans of chopped tomatoes

4 medium all-purpose (e.g. Wilja) potatoes, scrubbed and cut into 1 inch (2.5 cm) cubes

fromage frais and snipped fresh dill, to garnish

1 Put the onions, garlic, paprika, marjoram and ¹/₂ pint (300 ml) stock in a heavy-bottomed saucepan. Cover, bring to the boil, and boil for 5–7 minutes. Uncover and stir in the peppers. Simmer for a few minutes more until the mixture is very thick, the vegetables and paprika are 'frying' in their own juices, and the liquid is almost gone.

2 Stir in the remaining ingredients (except the fromage frais and dill), and add enough stock barely to cover the contents of the pan. Bring to the boil, then reduce the heat, cover and simmer, for 20–30 minutes or until the potatoes are tender. Serve in soup bowls garnished with a dollop of fromage frais and a sprinkling of snipped fresh dill.

Ⓥ Omit the fromage frais garnish

Turnip and Potato Stew

· · · · · · · · · · · · · · (V) · (Z) · · · · · · · · · · · · ·

Makes 2¹/₂ pints (1.4 litres)

Little white turnips have a delicately peppery flavour. They are lovely raw, as part of a crudité selection, but they also marry well with potatoes in a vegetable stew.

2 medium onions, halved and sliced into paper-thin half-moons.

3 garlic cloves, crushed

6 fl oz (175 ml) stock

3 small peppers (1 red, 1 yellow, 1 green), peeled, deseeded and sliced

3 small white turnips, coarsely diced

14 oz (400 g) can of tomatoes, drained and cut into strips

salt and freshly ground pepper

3 small all-purpose potatoes (e.g. Wilja), coarsely diced

3 tablespoons chopped fresh parsley

1 Put the onions, garlic and stock in a frying pan. Cover, bring to the boil, and boil for 3–4 minutes.

2 Uncover, reduce the heat slightly, and simmer briskly, stirring, until the onions are tender. Stir in the peppers and cook for a few minutes until they soften.

3 Stir in the turnips and tomatoes, and season with salt and pepper. Cover and simmer very gently for 10 minutes. Add the potatoes, re-cover and simmer until the turnips, potatoes and peppers are tender. Stir in the parsley.

Mushroom Ragout

· · · · · · · · · · · · · ·Ⓥ·Ⓩ· · · · · · · · · · · · · ·

Makes 1¹/₂ pints (900 ml)

The reconstituted dried mushrooms give this ragout resounding woodsy depths, but it is very good (if less intense) without them, too. The ragout fills a rice crust (see page 56) nicely, or a jacket potato, or a depression in a mound of mash. And it is the perfect partner for one of the foil-roasted vegetable gratins.

3–4 dried shiitake mushrooms

¹/₂ oz (15 g) dried *porcini* mushrooms

2 lb (900 g) mixed fresh mushrooms (white and brown caps), cut into quarters or eighths

6 spring onions, sliced

¹/₂ teaspoon dried tarragon, crumbled

2 fl oz (50 ml) dry sherry

several dashes of Teriyaki sauce

1 heaped tablespoon Dijon mustard

freshly ground pepper

1 Rinse the dried mushrooms under cold running water, then put them in a bowl and cover them with plenty of hot water. Leave to soak for 20 minutes.

2 Tip the dried mushrooms and soaking water through a sieve lined with a double thickness of muslin or coffee filter papers set over a bowl. Reserve mushrooms and soaking liquid.

3 Rinse the soaked mushrooms under cold running water, chop them coarsely (discarding the tough shiitake stems), and put them in a frying pan with the fresh mushrooms. Add 4 fl oz (100 ml) of the soaking liquid, the onions, tarragon, sherry and Teriyaki sauce. Cook, stirring occasionally, until the mushrooms have exuded a great deal of liquid.

4 Stir in the mustard, and season with pepper. Simmer until the mushrooms are tender and the liquid greatly reduced.

VARIATION

Creamy Mushroom Ragout

Stir a few spoonfuls of the mushroom soaking liquid or stock into 8 oz (225 g) ricotta cheese at room temperature. Fold this 'cream' into the Mushroom Ragout. Adjust the seasonings.

Roasted Root Vegetable Stew

· · · · · · · · · · · **V** · **Z** · · · · · · · · · · ·

Makes 2 ¹/₂ pints (1.4 litres)

A combination of roots, bulbs and stalks is roasted in an open pan and then enriched with a mustard, sherry and tarragon sauce. Peel and cube the sweet potato at the last minute; it turns dark if it sits around.

olive oil and water spray (see page 5)

1 head of garlic, cloves separated and peeled

1 mild onion, halved and cut into ¹/₂ inch (1 cm) wedges

1 fennel bulb, halved and cut into ¹/₂ inch (1 cm) slices

1 small (or ¹/₂ large) swede, peeled and cut into ¹/₂ inch (1 cm) pieces

1 large parsnip, cut into ¹/₂ inch (1 cm) pieces (if the core is tough and woody, cut it away)

2 carrots, cut into ¹/₂ inch (1 cm) slices

2 celery stalks, cut into ¹/₂ inch (1 cm) slices

1 medium sweet potato, cut into ¹/₂ inch (1 cm) pieces

¹/₂ pint (300 ml) stock

2–3 tablespoons medium dry sherry

¹/₂ teaspoon dried tarragon, crumbled

1 tablespoon Dijon mustard

2 tablespoons tomato purée

3–4 dashes of Teriyaki or soy sauce

juice of ¹/₂ large lemon

salt and freshly ground pepper

1 Preheat the oven to 450°F, 230°C, Gas Mark 8.

2 Lightly mist a wide, shallow baking dish with the oil spray. Spread all the vegetables in the dish and mist the vegetables lightly with the spray. Pour in ¹/₄ pint (150 ml) stock, and stir to combine everything. Bake, uncovered, in the oven for 30 minutes, stirring once or twice.

3 Pour the sherry into the dish, and stir and scrape with a wooden spoon to dislodge the browned bits on the bottom of the dish. Reduce the oven temperature to 350°F, 180°C, Gas Mark 4.

4 In a measuring jug, mix the remaining stock with the tarragon, mustard, tomato purée, Teriyaki or soy sauce and lemon juice. Stir into the stew and season with salt and pepper. Bake for a further 10–15 minutes.

Cauliflower Paprikash

. . . .

Makes 1 1/2 pints (900 ml)

Hungarian cuisine is one of the most interesting in the world, but the frequent appearance of lard or goose fat and soured cream make it one of the fattiest as well. The use of paprika (the ground dried pods of the red capsicum pepper) make the cuisine distinctive; the rosy blush of a paprika–soured cream sauce is a characteristic of many Hungarian dishes. In the first step of a Hungarian sauce, paprika, like curry spices, is always gently cooked in butter, lard or oil with the flavouring vegetables. Cook it gently in stock instead. Ricotta cheese stands in for cream, giving a delicious creaminess for a fraction of the fat content.

I large mild onion, chopped
I garlic clove, crushed
1/2 teaspoon dried marjoram, crumbled (optional)
2 carrots, chopped
2 red peppers, peeled, deseeded and chopped
2–3 dry-packed sun-dried tomatoes, chopped

I tablespoon paprika
1 1/4 pints (750 ml) stock
4 fl oz (100 ml) dry vermouth
I cauliflower, separated into florets
1/2 pint (300 ml) carton of passata
salt and freshly ground pepper
1 1/2 oz (40 g) ricotta cheese

1 Put the onion, garlic, marjoram (if using), carrots, peppers, sun-dried tomatoes, paprika, 1 pint (600 ml) stock and the vermouth in a flameproof casserole. Cover, bring to the boil, and boil for 5–7 minutes. Uncover, reduce the heat, and simmer until the vegetables and paprika are gently 'frying' in their own juices.

2 Stir in the cauliflower, passata and remaining stock. Season with salt and pepper, and simmer, partially covered, for 20–30 minutes or until the cauliflower is very tender, stirring occasionally.

3 Put the ricotta in a blender or food processor with a few spoonfuls of the sauce, and purée. Stir this creamy purée back into the casserole, and bring back to barely simmering. Taste, and adjust seasonings, if necessary.

Potatoes

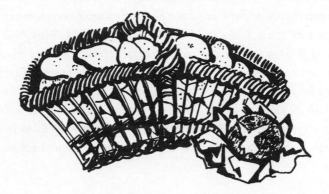

The potato, that starchy and delicious culinary wonder, is not just another vegetable. With its comforting, substantial and versatile qualities, it can centre a meal like nothing else.

Potatoes originated in the Andes of South America at least 8,000 years ago, and eventually became a significant staple – spiritual, economic and nutritional – of the Inca Empire. It wasn't until the exploration of the so-called New World that potatoes found their way to Europe. Much romantic folklore attributes the momentous introduction of the potato in Europe to Sir Walter Raleigh, or Sir Francis Drake, but it was most likely a nameless, but ethnobotanically curious, Spanish sailor who first brought the potato to European shores. Potatoes are so deeply entrenched in our food habits, that it is startling to realise that they have only been around since the sixteenth century. And they weren't exactly welcomed with open arms (or mouths) either. People throughout Europe refused to have anything to do with the strange tubers; they were believed to be evil, decadent, and as poisonous as their relative, deadly nightshade.

Times change. The only fear of potatoes people harbour these days is that spuds will make them fat. Nonsense! A potato contains virtually no fat, pretty good protein, and a nice package of fibre, vitamins and

minerals. Treat them right (don't douse them in high-fat ingredients) and potatoes will comfort and sustain you through a lifetime of happy and healthy eating.

Jacket Potatoes

The best jacket potatoes take time, in a hot oven. Preheat the oven to 425°F, 220°C, Gas Mark 7. Scrub the potatoes, then pierce in several places with a fork or thin skewer. Bake directly on the oven shelf for 1¼–1½ hours, turning once during baking. When done, the potatoes are creamy–fluffy on the inside and delightfully crunchy on the outside.

Always open your potatoes like this: with a fork, perforate the potato on top in a dotted 'X'. Then squeeze, so that the fluffy potato flesh surges up through the crunchy skin. If you use a knife to cut them open, instead of perforating with a fork and squeezing, the texture will be slightly lumpy, instead of the glorious fluffy, creamy, steamy texture that – against the crunchiness of the skin – makes a jacket potato such a pleasure to eat.

Jacket potatoes are delicious with freshly ground pepper, a squeeze of fresh lemon, a dollop of fromage frais or one of the dips, spreads, sauces or raitas in this book. A perfect, large jacket potato, overflowing with your chosen filling, makes a sustaining and delicious main course.

Opposite page 170, top to bottom Grilled Vegetable Mosaic (page 133), Potato-Wild Mushroom Gratin (page 177)

Clockwise from top Spicy Oven-Fried Potatoes (page 175), Mexican Salsa (page 186), filled tortillas (page 194), Black Beans (page 111), Green Pea Dip (page 37)

Baked Potato Halves

Baking potatoes in the microwave is fast, but you end up with steamed potatoes, quite different from the real crunchy-skinned, fluffy-fleshed thing. If you combine the microwave and the conventional oven you save quite a bit of time, yet the results are exemplary: potato halves that are as fluffy as mashed potatoes on the inside, as crunchy as chips on the outside. As with all recipes using the oven (both microwave and conventional), use the times as a guide only.

1 Preheat the conventional oven to its highest setting.

Halve two baking potatoes (I've done this, with excellent results, with Cara, Maris Piper and King Edward potatoes). Put a double sheet of absorbent kitchen paper on the microwave turntable. Place the potatoes, skin-side down, on the paper. Microwave on high (100%) for 5 minutes.

2 Turn the potatoes skin-side up, and microwave on high (100%) for another 5 minutes.

3 Place the potatoes directly on the shelf of the conventional oven, skin-side down, and bake for 10 minutes. Turn skin-side up and bake for another 10 minutes. When golden, puffed and cooked through, the potatoes are ready. Serve at once. Eat just as they are or serve with a dollop of Roasted Tomato Ketchup (see page 93) or Tomato Sauce (see pages 91–2) and a dollop of Creamy Herb Sauce (see page 192). Dip the potatoes into the two dollops, as you eat them.

Mashed Baked Potatoes

. . . .

To make exceptional mashed potatoes, bake them first (see page 171). Scoop the baked flesh out of the baked potatoes into a bowl. Mash well with an old-fashioned potato masher or – if you want it fluffier – push through a ricer. With a wooden spoon, beat in some fromage frais or buttermilk, and beat in a little grated Parmesan or medium-fat Cheddar along with salt and freshly ground pepper to taste. Pile the mash into a large bowl. Garnish around the edges with whatever takes your fancy: Mushroom Ragout (see page 167), Stir-Fried Peppers (see page 151), spinach. Or make a crater in the potatoes and fill with Green Split Pea Dhal (see page 113), Gravy (see page 94), one of the tomato or pepper sauces, Peperonata (see page 153) or Herbed Aubergine Sauce (see page 96). I'm sure you get the idea.

The advantages of the baked-potato method of making mashed spuds are twofold:

- *The quality of the mash is the best it can be.*

- *You have those seductive potato skins left over, just begging to be eaten. Eat them on the spot, or refrigerate them and save them for an indulgent snack. At snack time, cut them into strips, and grill, inside-up, for a few minutes (not too long) to crisp them. Grind on some pepper, and salt lightly, if you wish. Eat plain, or with a dip or sauce. Or make a light meal out of them: cut each whole potato skin into eight pieces, arrange inside-up on a baking sheet, fill each piece with a dab of tomato sauce, top with half-fat mozzarella and grill.*

Chips

· · · · · · · · · · · · · V · · · · · · · · · · · ·

With an atomiser oil and water spray (see page 5), a non-stick baking sheet and a hot oven, you can have chips that rival the real, boiled-in-oil thing. How nice to bite into a chip and taste potatoes – not a mouthful of grease! As with all oven recipes, adjust the time to suit your oven.

oil and water spray (see page 5)
baking potatoes (King Edward or
  Maris Piper are excellent)

1 Preheat the oven to 425°F, 220°C, Gas Mark 7.

2 Don't bother to peel the potatoes. Just scrub them and cut them across into $^1/_4$–$^1/_2$ inch (5 mm–1 cm) slices. Cut each slice in half.

3 You will need one or two flat non-stick baking sheets. Mist them lightly with the oil spray. Spread the potatoes on the sheet(s) in one layer, put them in the oven and leave them for 20–30 minutes.

4 Pull the potatoes out and gently turn them with a spatula. Return them to the oven for a further 15–25 minutes (the timing depends on the thickness of the slices, and on your oven). By this time, the 'chips' should be browned, crunchy on the outside and puffed. Serve at once.

NOTE

If you are using more than one baking sheet, you will need to switch their positions during baking, so that all the potato pieces bake evenly.

Spicy Oven-Fried Potatoes

Serves 2–4

For this spicy variation on oven chips, I like to use all-purpose potatoes instead of bakers. The piquant, crunchy little morsels are good hot or at room temperature, although it's hard to keep them around long enough to cool down. As a nibble with drinks, they are dandy.

½ teaspoon ground turmeric
½ teaspoon garam masala
¼ teaspoon ground cumin
a few drops of lemon juice
1 heaped tablespoon tomato purée

1 lb (450 g) all-purpose (e.g. Wilja) potatoes, peeled and cut into ½ inch (1 cm) cubes
olive oil and water spray (see page 5)

1 Preheat the oven to 425°F, 220°C, Gas Mark 7.

2 Whisk together the spices, lemon juice and tomato purée in a large bowl. With two spoons, toss the potato cubes with the spice and tomato mixture until very well coated.

3 Mist a non-stick baking sheet with the oil and water spray. Spread the potatoes out on the tray in one layer, and bake in the oven for 25–35 minutes, turning them once or twice. When they are browned, puffy and tender, they are ready.

Steam-Roasted Potatoes in Parchment Packets

· · · · · · · · · · · **V** · · · · · · · · · · · ·

Serves 1

If you wrap potato cubes in baking parchment and bake the parcels in a hot oven, the potatoes steam as they roast. The potato pieces that rest cut-side down on the parchment turn dark brown and smoky, those that rest skin-side up puff up with steam; the contrast is part of what makes these potatoes so spectacular. Serve as they are, or serve with Colombian Tomato–Cheese Sauce (see page 98), or any sauce you like.

4–5 new potatoes or 2–3 smallish all-purpose potatoes (e.g. Wilja)

olive oil and water spray (see page 5)

1 Preheat the oven to 425°F, 220°C, Gas Mark 7.

2 Scrub the potatoes and dry them. If you are using new potatoes, halve or quarter them. If you are using all-purpose potatoes, cut them into quarters or eighths. (You need potato pieces of about 1 inch/2.5 cm).

3 Tear off a piece of baking parchment large enough to enfold the potatoes generously. Fold the paper in half and crease it along the fold. Open and mist the paper lightly and evenly with the oil spray. Spread the potato pieces evenly on one half of the paper – some of them cut-side down, some skin-side down. Fold the other half of the paper over and seal securely by folding over and crimping the edges all round and forming a roughly semi-circular parcel (see page 127). The parcel should be roomy but well sealed. Slide the parcel on to a baking sheet, take it to the oven, then slide the parcel off the sheet, directly on to the oven shelf. Bake for 30–35 minutes or until the packets are puffy and the smoky aroma of roasting potatoes is driving everyone wild. Slide the parcel on to a platter and open by cutting a cross in the top. Serve at once.

Potato–Wild Mushroom Gratin

· · · · · · · · · · · · · · 🌾 · · · · · · · · · · · · · ·

Serves 2 – 4

Only ¹/₂ oz (15 g) dried porcini *mushrooms is needed to imbue this entire gratin with their wild, woodsy flavour. The top layer of potatoes becomes as crisp as potato crisps, while the under layers are meltingly tender.*

¹/₂ oz (15 g) dried *porcini*
  mushrooms
¹/₂ pint (300 ml) warm water
2 large all-purpose (e.g. Wilja)
  potatoes, 8 oz (225 g) each,
  scrubbed and sliced paper-thin

salt and freshly ground pepper
about 1 teaspoon vegetable
  bouillon powder

1 Preheat the oven to 400°F, 200°C, Gas Mark 6.

2 Rinse the mushrooms under cold running water, and then leave them to soak in the warm water for 20 minutes. Tip the mushrooms into a sieve lined with a double layer of muslin or coffee filter papers set over a bowl. Reserve the mushrooms and soaking liquid. Rinse the soaked mushrooms under cold running water, chop them with kitchen scissors and set aside.

3 Arrange a layer of overlapping potato slices on the bottom of a shallow baking dish that will hold the potatoes in three layers. Season with a little salt and pepper, and sprinkle evenly with half the mushrooms. Cover with another layer of potatoes, season, and sprinkle with the remaining mushrooms. Top with the remainder of the potatoes and season lightly with salt and pepper.

4 Stir the bouillon powder into the reserved mushroom liquid in a saucepan, and bring to the boil. Pour over the potatoes. Cover with foil (shiny side in) and bake in the oven for 15 minutes.

5 Uncover and bake for a further 30–40 minutes or until the liquid is absorbed, the under layers are meltingly tender (check with the tip of a small, sharp knife) and the top is crisp. Serve at once.

Potato Frittata

. . . .

Serves 2

Frittata is the Italian name for an open-faced omelette that can be filled with almost any savoury mixture. I have eliminated half of the egg yolks (see box), but if you have been told to curtail your dietary cholesterol drastically, it would be best to give this recipe a miss.

I large all-purpose (e.g. Wilja) potato, scrubbed and diced
I large onion, chopped
I garlic clove, crushed
1/2 pint (300 ml) stock
oil and water spray (see page 5)
2 eggs

2 egg whites
2–3 tablespoons chopped fresh parsley
salt and freshly ground pepper
2 tablespoons grated Parmesan, medium-fat Cheddar or Swiss cheese

1 Put the potato, onion, garlic and stock in an 8–10 inch (20.5–25.5 cm) non-stick frying pan. Bring to the boil, cover and boil for 5 minutes.

2 Uncover, reduce the heat and simmer until the stock is almost gone and the vegetables are tender. Scrape the mixture into a bowl, wipe out the pan, then mist with the oil spray.

3 Preheat the grill. Beat the eggs and the egg whites together with the parsley, and season with salt and pepper. Heat the pan and pour in the egg mixture. Cook over medium heat, without stirring, for a few seconds or until the eggs begin to set on the bottom, then spoon in the potato mixture.

4 With a flexible plastic spatula, lift the edges of the omelette away from the pan, and tilt the pan so that the uncooked egg flows beneath the cooked portion. Continue doing this all around the pan until the omelette is almost completely set.

5 Sprinkle the top of the omelette with cheese. Flash under the grill for 2–3 minutes to set, melt the cheese, and very lightly brown the top. Serve at once, in wedges, straight from the pan.

WHAT TO DO WITH LEFTOVER EGG YOLKS

1 Feed them to your dog. Dogs metabolise fat and cholesterol differently from humans. The yolks will make your dog's coat shine.

2 Find a book on natural beauty remedies (Anita Guyton, *The Natural Guide to Beauty*, published by Thorsons and available from libraries, is excellent) and learn how to make egg yolk hair and skin lotions.

3 Make egg tempera from the yolks, and paint beautiful pictures (see an artist's manual for directions).

Potato–Fennel Gratin

. . . . **V** . . . .

Serves 2–4

Substitute fennel for the porcini *used in the recipe on page 177, and the potatoes take on a gentle anise character.*

2 all-purpose (e.g. Wilja) potatoes, 8 oz (225 g) each, scrubbed and sliced paper-thin
2 fennel bulbs, trimmed and cut across into paper-thin slices

about ½ pint (300 ml) boiling stock
freshly ground pepper

1 Preheat the oven to 400°F, 200°C, Gas Mark 6.

2 Arrange overlapping rows of potato slices and fennel slices in a single layer in a gratin dish. Pour 8 fl oz (225 ml) hot stock evenly over the vegetables, season with pepper and cover with foil, shiny-side in.

3 Bake in the oven for 15 minutes. Uncover and bake for a further 15–25 minutes or until the vegetables are tender, brushing the potatoes with stock (use a pastry brush) occasionally during the last 5–10 minutes.

Potato Chilli

· ·

Makes 2 pints (1.1 litres)

Chilli doesn't have to be con carne! – *it can be* con patate, *as well. This dish can be made ahead of time, and reheated at serving time; the flavour will only improve, although you may have to thin it with a bit of stock before reheating.*

about 1 pint (600 ml) stock

3 large onions, halved and sliced into thin half-moons

2 garlic cloves, crushed

1 teaspoon each of dried oregano (crumbled), ground coriander, mild chilli powder and ground cumin

1 tablespoon paprika

cayenne pepper, to taste

3 heaped tablespoons tomato purée

3 large all-purpose (e.g. Wilja) potatoes, scrubbed, halved and cut into 1½ inch (4 cm) chunks

salt and freshly ground pepper

grated Parmesan or medium fat Cheddar cheese and fromage frais, to serve

PEPPER SALAD

3 large peppers (1 red, 1 yellow, 1 green), peeled, deseeded and diced

3 thin spring onions, sliced

1 tablespoon chopped fresh parsley

½ tablespoon chopped fresh coriander

juice of 1 lime

salt

½ teaspoon sugar

1 Put ½ pint (300 ml) of the stock in a flameproof casserole with the onions, garlic, herbs and spices. Cover, bring to the boil, and boil for 10 minutes.

2 Uncover and cook for 5–7 minutes or until the onions are tender and the liquid has almost cooked away. Blend in the tomato purée.

3 Stir the potatoes into the onion mixture, season with salt and pepper, then pour in the remaining stock. Bring to a simmer, stirring. Partially cover and simmer for 45–55 minutes or until the potatoes are tender and the sauce is very thick and rich.

4 Meanwhile, to make the pepper salad, toss all the ingredients together in a bowl at least 30 minutes before serving.

5 Serve the chilli in shallow soup bowls. Top each serving with a sprinkling of cheese, a dollop of fromage frais, and a spoonful of pepper salad.

❰❱ Without the cheese or fromage frais garnish.

Colourful Potato–Vegetable Casserole

. . . . ❰❱ . . . .

Makes 3¹/₂ pints (2 litres)

It's not necessary to peel the potatoes, but the peppers – as always – are much improved if peeled. This casserole is exceptionally aromatic.

5 medium all-purpose (e.g. Wilja) potatoes, 4 oz (100 g) each, scrubbed and thickly sliced

2 medium onions, halved and sliced into thick half-moons

2 large yellow peppers, peeled, and cut into 1 inch (2.5 cm) chunks

3 celery stalks, cut into 2 inch (5 cm) pieces

1 fennel bulb, cut into eighths

two 14 oz (400 g) cans of Italian peeled tomatoes, well drained and crushed with the fingers

1 fresh chilli, deseeded and chopped

a handful of basil leaves, shredded

2 tablespoons finely chopped fresh parsley

salt and freshly ground pepper

olive oil and water spray (see page 5)

1 Preheat the oven to 450°F, 230°C, Gas Mark 8.

2 Put the potatoes and onions in a bowl, add all the remaining ingredients, except the oil spray, and toss to mix. Mist lightly with the oil spray and toss once more. Spread the mixture in a gratin dish and cover tightly with foil.

3 Bake in the oven for 45–50 minutes or until the potatoes, celery and fennel are very tender.

Smoked Tofu and Potato Salad

V

Makes 2¹/₂ pints (1.4 litres)

Potato salads are usually dressed in one of two ways: with a vinaigrette or with mayonnaise. In place of vinaigrette, try an infusion of stock, sun-dried tomatoes and garlic, combined with balsamic vinegar as in this recipe. In the two recipes following this one, fromage frais stands in nicely for mayonnaise.

1¹/₂ lb (700 g) new potatoes, scrubbed

8 oz (225 g) smoked tofu, cubed

1 tablespoon capers, drained

1 grilled pepper (see page 131), deseeded and diced (roasted peppers from a jar or can may be used) or 1 fresh red pepper, peeled, deseeded and diced

2 tablespoons balsamic vinegar

¹/₂ pint (300 ml) stock

3–4 dry-packed sun-dried tomatoes, finely diced (use scissors)

1–2 pinches of crushed dried chillies

1 garlic clove, crushed

freshly ground pepper

2 tablespoons chopped fresh parsley

3 spring onions, cut in half lengthways, then thinly sliced across

1 Steam the potatoes over boiling water until tender but not falling apart. Halve or quarter them.

2 While the potatoes are still warm, gently toss them with the smoked tofu, capers and peppers in a bowl. Add the balsamic vinegar and toss well.

3 Put the stock, tomatoes, chilli and garlic in a small frying pan. Bring to the boil, and boil rapidly until the liquid is reduced by half. Immediately pour the stock mixture over the potatoes. With two wooden spoons, gently turn the potatoes so that they are coated with the stock mixture. Season with pepper. Mix in the parsley and spring onions just before serving.

Spicy Potato Salad

· ·

Makes 2¹/₂ pints (1.4 litres)

The secret of this potato salad and the next, is lime juice, Teriyaki sauce, and lively seasonings added to the potatoes while they are still warm, so the flavour penetrates right through. Finally, fold in the creamy fromage frais dressing.

1¹/₂ lb (700 g) boiling or all-purpose (e.g. Wilja) potatoes, scrubbed

2 tablespoons fresh lime or lemon juice

1 teaspoon Teriyaki sauce

1–2 pinches of cayenne pepper (optional)

¹/₂ teaspoon ground cumin

2 celery stalks, diced

1 carrot, coarsely grated

1 red pepper, peeled, deseeded and diced

salt and freshly ground pepper

DRESSING

5 tablespoons very low-fat fromage frais

3 spring onions, thinly sliced

1 tablespoon snipped fresh chives

1 tablespoon chopped fresh parsley

1 Steam the potatoes over boiling water until tender but not mushy.

2 Meanwhile, to make the dressing, combine all the ingredients thoroughly.

3 While still warm, cut the potatoes into 1 inch (2.5 cm) cubes and transfer to a bowl. Add the lime or lemon juice, Teriyaki sauce and spices, and toss well.

4 Add all the remaining ingredients and the dressing and toss gently to combine.

Chick Pea and Potato Salad

Makes 2¹/₂ pints (1.4 litres)

Potatoes and chick peas make good companions, particularly in a salad. Serve garnished with one of the tomato relishes (see pages 187–9) for beautiful colour.

1 lb (450 g) boiling potatoes, scrubbed

15 oz (432 g) can of chick peas, drained and rinsed

2 tablespoons fresh lime juice

1 teaspoon Teriyaki sauce

¹/₂ teaspoon ground cumin

3 spring onions, thinly sliced

2 tablespoons chopped fresh parsley

4 tablespoons fromage frais

1 Steam the potatoes over boiling water until tender but not mushy. When cool enough to handle, cut into ¹/₂ inch (1 cm) cubes and transfer to a bowl.

2 Add the chick peas to the potatoes. Stir together the lime juice, Teriyaki sauce and cumin, and pour over the potatoes and chick peas. Toss gently with two spoons so that they absorb the liquid. Stir in the spring onions and parsley. Allow to cool.

3 Finally, gently fold the fromage frais into the salad.

Relishes, Raitas, Salsas and Chutneys

These are the extra little fillips that provide the final note of texture, flavour and colour to a vegetarian meal; the crowning touch to an already bursting-with-personality repast. Most of them are very quick to throw together; make several at once, and keep in the fridge (in covered containers) to embellish your meals.

Carrot Sultana Chutney

· · · · · · · · · · · · · V · · · · · · · · · · · ·

Makes 1 pint (600 ml)

You might find yourself eating this simple and refreshing chutney straight out of its container, and why not? It will keep in the fridge for 3–4 days.

6 large carrots, about 1 lb (450 g), grated

4 tablespoons sultanas

4 tablespoons chopped fresh parsley

2 tablespoons shredded fresh mint

1/2 teaspoon ground cumin

juice of 2 large lemons and 2 large oranges

1 Put the grated carrots in a lidded container, and add the sultanas, parsley and mint.

2 Stir the cumin into the citrus juices, then add to the carrots. Cover the container and shake well to combine thoroughly. Chill for at least 1 hour before using.

Mexican Salsa

· · · · · · · · · · · · · V · · · · · · · · · · · ·

Makes 3 pints (1.7 litres)

A Mexican salsa is used as a salad, relish or sauce. It's great as a zesty garnish to beans and vegetable chillies, and it's good as a dip with pita crisps or tortilla chips, or as a relish in pita pocket sandwiches or wrapped tortillas. It improves with age, so make it ahead of time and let it mellow. The chilli and garlic can be increased or eliminated according to your taste. This salsa will keep in the fridge for 4–5 days.

two 1³/₄ lb (800 g) cans of Italian
  tomatoes, well drained
14 oz (400 g) can or jar of red
  peppers, well drained, or 2–3
  grilled peppers (see page 131),
  or peeled raw peppers
1 fresh chilli (or less to taste),
  deseeded and chopped

2 fl oz (50 ml) red wine vinegar
1–2 garlic cloves, crushed
2 tablespoons chopped fresh
  parsley
2 tablespoons chopped fresh
  mint

1 Crush the tomatoes with your fingers and put in a bowl. Dice the peppers with kitchen scissors and add to the tomatoes. Add all the remaining ingredients and mix well.

Tomato Sweetcorn Relish

· · · · · · · · · · · · · · · **V** · · · · · · · · · · · · · ·

Makes 1¹/₂ pints (900 ml)

Sweetcorn survives processing very well – frozen corn is excellent, and canned corn is good, too. Use whichever is most convenient. This is another of those compelling salad relishes you will want to eat straight out of the container. It will keep in the fridge for 4–5 days.

8 oz (225 g) frozen sweetcorn
  kernels, cooked briefly and
  drained
9 oz (250 g) cherry tomatoes,
  quartered
2 grilled peppers (see page 131),
  deseeded or use canned
  peppers (pimentos)
1 fresh chilli, deseeded and finely
  chopped

salt and freshly ground pepper
2 fl oz (50 ml) balsamic vinegar
1 tablespoon caster sugar
2 tablespoons each of chopped
  fresh coriander, chopped fresh
  parsley and snipped fresh
  chives

1 Put all the ingredients together in a bowl, and toss until the sugar is dissolved.

2 Spoon into a jar or container, cover and refrigerate until needed.

Cherry Tomato and Cucumber Relish

V

Makes 2 pints (1.1 litres)

The trick to good-tasting cherry tomatoes is to buy them several days before you use them, so that their flavour has time to develop. Don't refrigerate them, or the flavour never arrives. The sweetness and deep tomato character of most cherry tomatoes make them perfect for snacking. I keep a bowl of them out on the kitchen counter at all times, and they disappear very fast. This relish is best eaten on the day it is made, but will keep for a day or so.

18 oz (500 g) cherry tomatoes, quartered

1 large cucumber, peeled, halved lengthways, deseeded and thinly sliced

1 fresh chilli, deseeded and finely chopped

1 tablespoon small capers, drained

2 teaspoons brine from jar of capers

1½ teaspoons balsamic vinegar

1–2 garlic cloves, crushed (optional)

juice of ½ lime

3 spring onions, thinly sliced

2 tablespoons chopped fresh parsley

2 tablespoons chopped fresh coriander

2 tablespoons shredded fresh mint

freshly ground pepper

1 Put all the ingredients together in a bowl and mix well. Leave to stand at room temperature until serving time, stirring occasionally.

Tomato and Watercress Relish

· · · · · · · · · · · · · ◊ · · · · · · · · · · · · ·

Makes 6 halves

Simple, simple, simple, but very effective as to colour and taste.
Amounts don't really matter, just throw it together — you can't go
wrong. This relish does not keep well, so use on the day it is made.

cherry tomatoes (a mixture of
   red and yellow, if you can find
   them)
watercress

snipped fresh chives or thinly
   sliced spring onions
salt

1 Halve the cherry tomatoes and place in a bowl.

2 Steam the watercress over boiling water for 10 seconds. Immediately rinse well under cold running water, and shake dry. Trim off any woody stems, and cut or tear the remaining stems and leaves into 1 inch (2.5 cm) pieces. Add to the tomatoes.

3 Add the chives or spring onions and toss the mixture together. Leave to stand for about 1 hour. Just before serving, salt lightly and toss again.

Fruit and Fennel Chutney

· · · · · · · · · · · · · **V** · · · · · · · · · · · ·

Makes ³/₄ pint (450 ml)

I couldn't resist reprinting this wonderful, fruity chutney from Slim Cuisine, Quick and Easy. It's the combination of fragrant, juicy mango with anise-flavoured, crisp fennel, spiked with a touch of chilli, that makes it so memorable. It will keep for 2–3 days.

1 orange, peeled and diced
1 ripe mango, diced (see box)
1 fennel bulb, diced
½ small fresh chilli, deseeded and finely chopped, or to taste (optional)
1 tablespoon chopped fresh mint

1 tablespoon chopped fresh parsley
4 tablespoons orange juice
2 tablespoons lime juice
salt and freshly ground pepper

❙ Put all the ingredients together in a bowl and mix well. Refrigerate until needed.

PREPARING MANGOES

To dice a mango, use a sharp knife to cut the mango as if you were slicing it in half, but cutting just to one side of the large, flat central stone. Slice down again on the other side of the stone. You will now have two half mangoes and the flat centre stone to which quite a bit of mango flesh still clings.

With a small, sharp paring knife, score each mango half lengthways and crossways, cutting through the flesh all the way to, but not through, the skin. Push out the skin as if you were pushing the mango half inside out. The mango flesh will stand out in cubes. Slice these cubes off the skin.

Peel the skin from the centre slice left on the stone. Either slice the mango flesh off the stone and use the trimmings in the chutney, or close the door, tie a tea-towel around your neck, lean over the kitchen sink, and gnaw the juicy mango flesh off the stone. It's messy, succulent, and utterly delicious – it's the cook's reward.

Mint and Coriander Raita

· ·

Makes ¹/₂ pint (300 ml)

Raitas are cooling mixtures of yoghurt, herbs and seasonings, meant to accompany curries. I use very low-fat fromage frais instead of yoghurt, because it is much thicker and creamier than low-fat yoghurt. The three raitas that follow work well as garnishes for vegetable stews (see pages 156–69), or as dips or salad dressings. Depending on which herbs you use, the raitas can work with almost anything, not just curries. If the fromage frais is fresh, raita will keep in the fridge for 4–5 days.

¹/₂ pint (300 ml) very low-fat fromage frais

4 spring onions, sliced

¹/₂ inch (1 cm) piece of fresh root ginger, peeled and crushed

1 fresh green chilli, deseeded and chopped (optional)

4 tablespoons shredded fresh mint leaves

6 tablespoons chopped fresh coriander

1 Put all the ingredients together in a bowl and mix well. Cover and refrigerate until required.

Cucumber Raita

· ·

Makes 3 pints (1.7 litres)

Cucumber Raita is very cooling, and the texture is wonderful. It makes a great dip or spread, as well as a curry accompaniment.

2 large cucumbers

salt

1 garlic clove, crushed

2 tablespoons white wine vinegar

¹/₂ pint (300 ml) very low-fat fromage frais

3 spring onions, sliced

2 tablespoons chopped fresh parsley

2 tablespoons shredded fresh mint

¹/₂ teaspoon ground cumin

¹/₂ teaspoon ground coriander

freshly ground pepper

1 Peel the cucumbers and cut them in half lengthways. With a teaspoon, scoop out the seeds from each half and discard them. Cut the cucumber halves into slices about ¼ inch (5 mm) thick. Toss with a little salt and leave in a non-reactive colander to drain for 30 minutes.

2 While the cucumbers are draining, put the garlic and wine vinegar in a non-reactive bowl, and leave to marinate.

3 Rinse the cucumbers and dry very well with absorbent kitchen paper. Stir into the garlic and wine vinegar mixture. Fold in the fromage frais, then fold in all remaining ingredients. Taste and adjust the seasonings. Cover and refrigerate until required.

Creamy Herb Sauce

. . . .

This is a sort of all-purpose raita that will go nicely with a wide variety of dishes, depending on which herbs you choose to use.

very low-fat fromage frais
shredded, chopped or snipped
    fresh herbs (good combinations
    are mint and coriander, mint
    and dill, chives and parsley,
    thyme and tarragon, oregano
    and basil. Or try using just one
    herb at a time.)

1 Whisk the fromage frais and add a generous amount of a single fresh herb or a combination of herbs. Cover and store in the fridge until needed.

VEGAN RAITA

Purée silken tofu in a blender with herbs and seasonings (see Cucumber Raita recipe), to make a creamy non-dairy raita.

Wrap-Ups

Filo is a paper-thin, low-fat pastry available in boxes, chilled or frozen, from supermarkets. Traditionally, filo is prepared by arranging the paper-thin sheets in layers, liberally buttering or oiling between the layers. As a result, most filo dishes are not low-fat choices. However, for a lower-fat version, each layer can be brushed with lightly beaten egg (or egg white, if you must drastically curtail your cholesterol) or – for vegans, *lightly* misted with oil and water spray (see page 5). Prepared this way, filo makes an excellent low-fat wrapping for vegetarian 'sausage' rolls, or for little samosa-like turnovers.

Tortillas

Makes 6 halves

Tortillas are flat Mexican pancakes, made of maize or wheat. Suddenly, they can be found on supermarket shelves, side by side with the packaged bread. With a stack of tortillas, and a can or two of beans, wonderful meal possibilities lie in store. Here's how to do it:

If you are not going to use the tortillas within a few days of purchase, store them in the freezer, in their wrapper. To prepare (they just need warming), wrap the tortillas (a mixture of maize and wheat, if possible) in foil and warm in a steamer over boiling water for about 5 minutes, or in the oven at 350°F, 180°C, Gas Mark 4 for 10 minutes. (Add an extra 5 minutes if preparing from frozen.) Wrap the warm tortillas in a clean tea-towel or napkin and put on a plate or in a basket. Serve with bowls of beans – Spicy Bean Dip (see page 42), Zesty Beans (see page 105), or Black Beans (see page 111) – along with Mexican Salsa (see page 186), Green Pea Dip (see page 37), Creamy Herb Sauce (see page 192), and brown rice. Have in bowls, as well, shredded half-fat mozzarella (or you could add cubed mozzarella to the bowl of hot beans so the cubes form molten lumps – marvellous!), chopped fresh chilli, and sliced spring onions. Let everyone spoon combinations of the beans and accompaniments into their tortillas, wrap and eat (supply plenty of paper napkins).

ⓥ Substitute cubes of smoked tofu for the mozzarella

'Sausage' Rolls

· · · · · · · · · · · · · ⓩ · · · · · · · · · · · · ·

Makes 12 rolls

Suitable fillings for these include Lentil 'Bolognese' Sauce (see page 97) with some breadcrumbs added to bind it. Duxelles (see page 36) is excellent as well (no breadcrumbs needed). The rolls can be prepared up to the end of step 3, and then frozen. To bake from frozen, add 5 minutes to the baking time.

1 14 oz (400 g) package filo pastry, thawed if frozen	filling of your choice (see above)
1 egg, lightly beaten	oil and water spray (see page 5)

1 Preheat the oven to 400°F, 200°C, Gas Mark 6.

2 Put a piece of cling film on your work surface. Unwrap and unroll the filo (a package will contain about 12 sheets), put it on the cling film, and cover well with another piece of cling film. (The pastry will dry out quickly if left uncovered, so keep covered at all times.)

3 Remove a single sheet of filo from the stack, and spread it flat on the work surface. Lightly brush it with beaten egg, leaving a 1 inch (2.5 cm) border all around. Spread 1 tablespoon of the filling in a strip where the egg wash begins along one short side. Roll the pastry around the filling, and continue rolling it up to form a tube shape. Crimp and twist the ends of the tube to give it a Christmas-cracker shape. Don't wrap too tightly, because the filling will expand a bit while baking. Put, seam-side down, on a *non-stick* baking sheet that you have misted lightly with oil and water spray. Mist the top of the 'cracker' lightly with oil and water spray. Repeat until the filo and filling are used up.

4 Bake in the oven for 10–15 minutes or until golden brown, sizzling and puffed. Check once during baking: shake the tray, and if any rolls seem to be sticking, loosen them with a spatula or palette knife and change their position.

Samosas

. . . . ⓩ . . . .

Makes 12

Any of the vegetable curries or chillies on pages 156–65 make good fillings for these samosas, as does Duxelles (see page 36). The fillings used to stuff Cabbage Parcels (see page 118) and Spinach–Rice Pie (see page 56) are both fine, too. At the end of step 3, the samosas can be wrapped and refrigerated for a day or two, or frozen for months. To bake from frozen, add an extra 5 minutes to the baking time.

1 package filo pastry, thawed if frozen
1 egg, lightly beaten

oil and water spray (see page 5)
filling of your choice (see above)

1 Preheat the oven to 375°F, 190°C, Gas Mark 5.

2 Put a piece of cling film on your work surface. Unwrap and unroll the fillo (a package will contain about 12 sheets), put it on the cling film, and cover with a second piece of cling film. (The pastry will dry out quickly if left uncovered, so keep covered at all times.)

3 Take one piece of filo from the stack and spread it out on a work surface. Lightly brush the sheet with beaten egg. Fold the bottom third of the pastry up, and then the top third down, as if folding a business letter (see illustration opposite). Brush again with egg. Place a generous tablespoon of filling on the lower right-hand corner, and fold the top right-hand corner down to cover it and to form a triangle. Brush with more beaten egg. Fold the triangle over to form a new triangle, and brush with egg again. Continue folding and brushing lightly until you have formed a many-layered triangle. Mist the finished triangle lightly with oil spray and place on a *non-stick* baking sheet that you have misted lightly with oil spray. Make more samosas until all the pastry sheets and filling are used up.

4 Bake in the oven for 20–30 minutes or until puffed up and golden. Serve at once.

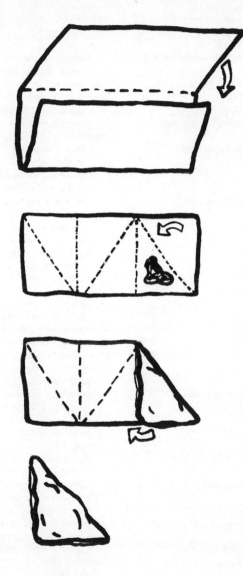

Index